M000233165

FAMILIARS
WITCHCRAFT

"In *Familiars in Witchcraft,* Maja D'Aoust brings together a vast wealth of lore, history, and incredibly useful insights with such readability and grace. In a subject cloaked in mystery, the author reveals her life experience and devoted education in what should be considered essential reading for the serious occultist and seeker alike."

GABRIEL DEAN ROBERTS, AUTHOR OF
THE QUEST FOR GNOSIS

"Maja D'Aoust has a unique talent for taking esoteric subjects and presenting them in a way that is lucid and insightful to the contemporary mind. *Familiars in Witchcraft* is useful to both scholars of the occult and the un-*familiar.*"

BRIAN MCGREEVY, AUTHOR OF
HEMLOCK GROVE

"Maja D'Aoust writes from the depth of her personal experience and never offers simple opinions or conjecture on her subject matter. Instead, what she gives us is background and evidence. Maja is not only a visionary practitioner but also a scholar with an oracle's ability to draw out what's important. The magic of *Familiars in Witchcraft,* and all of Maja's writing, is the way she pulls knowledge from the vast well of history and presents it to us in a clear, modern, conversational tone. After years of public lecturing, Maja is able to present ideas that can often seem arcane or impenetrable in a way that seems almost effortless. Her work serves as a bridge for lost or ancient wisdom, making it useful and accessible for the reader today."

RON REGÉ JR., AUTHOR OF
THE CARTOON UTOPIA

FAMILIARS IN
WITCHCRAFT

Supernatural Guardians in the Magical Traditions of the World

MAJA D'AOUST

Destiny Books
Rochester, Vermont

Destiny Books
One Park Street
Rochester, Vermont 05767
www.DestinyBooks.com

Text stock is SFI certified

Destiny Books is a division of Inner Traditions International

Copyright © 2019 by Maja D'Aoust

Cataloging-in-Publication Data for this title is available from the Library of Congress

ISBN 978-1-62055-846-1 (print)
ISBN 978-1-62055-847-8 (ebook)

Printed and bound in the United States by Lake Book Manufacturing, Inc. The text stock is SFI certified. The Sustainable Forestry Initiative® program promotes sustainable forest management.

10   9   8   7   6   5   4   3   2   1

Text design and layout by Virginia Scott Bowman
This book was typeset in Garamond Premier Pro with Putnam and Tide Sans used as display typefaces

To send correspondence to the author of this book, mail a first-class letter to the author c/o Inner Traditions • Bear & Company, One Park Street, Rochester, VT 05767, and we will forward the communication, or contact the author directly at **www.witchofthedawn.com**.

*This work is dedicated to and inspired by conversations
with my familiar guardian spirit; Dr. Kelvin DeWolfe;
Baza Novic for inspiration and research assistance;
Jon Graham for his support and art;
Myla Owl for her Magic; and Brooke Schooles
for her help in assembly of the manuscript.*

Contents

1

The Witch's Familiar

Same seeks same; we search out the familiar.
JILL ALEXANDER ESSBAUM, *HAUSFRAU*

One of the most romantic notions of the poets is the idea of a soul mate. Finding someone in this world who understands us implicitly and will love us forever and ever no matter what is a comforting sentiment. On an inherent soul level that kind of love is something everyone has longed for at some point, mostly when we are feeling isolated and alien, unloved and unwanted.

The soul mate has captured the imagination of countless individuals who pine and long for a relationship of this deep nature at some point during their life. The first to coin this term was the poet Samuel Taylor Coleridge in a letter in 1822: "In order not to be miserable, *you* must have a *Soul*-mate as well as a *House* or a *Yoke*-mate."[1] Here he meant that if all our relations are only mundane we will not be fulfilled to our potential. The soul mate is generally thought to be something deeply connected to you through some magical, fated string of providence in the woven blanket of time and space. When most people think of a soul mate, they think of a person, and more specifically a lover or romantic partner. But what many people feel uncomfortable recognizing is that almost every primitive culture has stories of animal and plant soul mates, or nonhuman spiritual soul mates and counterparts

1

as well as soul mates who are spirits of the dead. These are most widely known as familiar spirits. The soul mate has taken a multitude of forms in ancient versions of this entity and wasn't nearly as restrictive as our modern conceptions. Many tales of the saints address their forming a special soul mate relationship with a mountain, tree, or even a flower. Some Buddhist scholars have put forth that Siddhartha Buddha formed a spiritual link with the Bodhi Tree he sat under to claim his enlightenment. Some researchers feel it was the tree that instructed him on how to attain his Buddhahood, like a kind of assistant or mentor. The ancient religion of the Celtic Druids held similar beliefs, that trees could educate, inspire, and love humans, and many Native American tribes claim trees as their ancestors, listing them in their family lineages.

The concept of a special bond with an animal or natural thing symbolizes a bond with the world beyond humanity. Cities and geographical features, such as hills and rivers, are said to have familiar spirits, as well as stars and other celestial bodies. Many ancient cultures taught that through the unification of consciousness with animals or other living things in nature, humans enable their consciousness to unite with a larger living force—that of nature itself. When our consciousness unites with this force and we begin to identify with things other than human, our concept of what we are can powerfully grow out of our ego limitations. Imagine if a soul mate who loved you unconditionally could be something other than human. The amazing scientist Nikola Tesla, who never married, claimed that his soul mate was a pigeon whom he fed every day in the park. He loved the bird dearly. A soul mate can also be a spirit or supernatural being, and by relating to and identifying with such a familiar, we can widen our horizons, go beyond our limitations. A type of relationship between human beings and either animal, nature, or supernatural spirits is mentioned at some point in all ancient cultures and is not particular to witches. That this captivating concept of a soul mate, or a higher spirit level of relating, extends so deeply into humanity suggests that it is either a real phenomenon or simply an inherent need within us seeking expression.

What exactly is a familiar spirit, and why is it called familiar?

Witch with familiars
Original art by Maja D'Aoust

It is helpful to examine the etymology of the word *familiar*. This word comes from the Latin *famulus,* which is also where we get the word *family*. The word *famulus* means "servant," or more specifically a female servant who leads a household through her indentured devotion. This definition of family takes on new meaning when we look at the traditional role of the female housewife as bound to her duty. Similar in meaning to the word *famulus,* the word *doula* also means "female servant," or literally "slave," and describes a woman who acts as an assistant or servant to the woman giving birth in the family. Both words have a connotation of devotional servitude, and it is here that we gain insight into the role of the familiar spirit, which is to serve or provide a service to its bonded human. The familiar acts almost like a spiritual midwife for its human counterpart.

The familiar then is a kind of servant to the person with whom it is connected. It is hard not to recognize the hierarchical implications of this idea. The familiar seems more like Dobby the house elf from Harry Potter under this definition. The concept of humans having servants or being assisted by other beings, spirits, and creatures of the Earth is an old one, found in myths and scriptures.

We can certainly see the idea of humans "ruling" over nature in the Judeo-Christian Bible. Under many interpretations of the creation story it seems that Earth is for humans to rule over. In Genesis, Adam earns the privilege of naming all the things on Earth, and through his ability to name them he gains dominion over them.[2] Through this dominion, the creatures of the Earth served Adam and Eve. In reality humans use animals as a kind of slave, or servant, all the time—all we need to do is look to the ox pulling a cart for evidence of this. Using animals for work or food is the most common way that humans enslave them for their purposes as servants.

The ancient Egyptians had very sophisticated techniques of animal husbandry.[3] The domestication of cattle is personified or symbolized by the gods; for example, Hathor, the Egyptian cow goddess, taught humankind to calm and castrate the wild bull so that people might use its strength to plow the fields. Even the word *domestic* relates back to the concept of family and home, and the ability to domesticate an animal is really to make them one of us and allow them to enter into our domicile. This is also where we get the word *dominate*,[4] an important consideration since if you were to domesticate an animal you would have to find a strategy to ensure that it would not attack you. The process of domesticating a natural creature to serve the family implicates human lordship over the animal.

This is an important point that cannot be understated. If you lose control of your dog and it bites you or someone else, there are terrible consequences. Likewise, if you lose control of your familiar spirit and it goes feral, there can be similar dangers. Keeping trust and control when working with spirits can prevent mutiny. In the tales of King Solomon, for example, he was said to control spirits through the use of his ring— and when he lost that ring, by being tricked by the demon Asmodeus, the spirits with whom he was working attacked him mercilessly.[5]

This would be in keeping with the concept of the familiar as an animal servant; much like Adam domesticated the animals by naming them, the witch gains the servitude of the familiar through a special type of taming bond. In *Shamanism: Archaic Techniques of Ecstasy*, Mircea Eliade writes, "A relation of 'familiarity' is established between the shaman and his 'spirits.' And in fact, in ethnological literature they are known as 'familiar,' 'helping,' 'assistant,' or 'guardian' spirits."[6]

The bond formed between the domesticated spirit and the witch is one of trust. It is a relationship based on an understanding and an exchange of services. Familiar spirits can also be literally "family" spirits, because they can take the form of dead relatives. Ancestors play a huge role in the identity of many familiar spirits around the globe, and the worship of the dead while keeping relations with them is a highly practiced form of divination. Some of the religious institutions such as Taoism and Hinduism advocate feats of self-domination, such as fasting and abstinence, to attract the more powerful familiars. For when we become rulers and dominators of ourselves, we attract those willing to serve and follow us. Few soldiers would be willing to follow a general into battle who might break down and cry if you stepped on his toe. If you are looking to wrangle a powerful spirit, you would do well to begin a discipline of self-control, just as if you were seeking to raise and rear a child.

THE WITCH'S MARK

To his good friends thus wide I'll ope my arms;
And, like the kind life-rendering pelican,
Repast them with my blood.

WILLIAM SHAKESPEARE, *HAMLET*

The relationship with the soul mate familiar spirit usually included some type of exchange. Some of the things exchanged between the familiar and its host included food, sex, worship, and actions or deeds carried out at the instruction of the spirit's influence.

Sometimes meals were left on altars for the spirits of dead ancestors. This custom is a big part of the ritual of the Day of the Dead, which is prevalent throughout Mexico and other parts of South America. If you wanted one of your ancestor spirits to guard you and protect you, the best thing to do was to give it food. Different traditions provided different kinds of food for the spirits. In some places wheat was favored; other areas said that the spirits preferred sweets or alcohol. For millennia the preferred spirit food worldwide was blood. Blood and human sacrifice were thought to attract powerful spirits; spirits fed blood or offered animal or human sacrifices granted more power to the supplicants. Belief in blood offerings turned from the blood of the one calling the spirit to a scapegoat, or stand in, to provide the blood food. Though this may seem like a heathen activity, many scapegoat-type sacrifices were performed in Judaism, and during every communion held in Christian churches the blood of the scapegoat Jesus is offered up in sacrifice. Participation in blood sacrifices is still very widespread in modern cultures and religions, so to view it as some archaic primitive practice is only ignorance of current events. In African cultures, the blood was offered as part of the meal; the people ate the meat, but the blood was reserved for the spirits. Humans were not permitted to consume the blood as it was the food of the gods and so taboo. Jesus stated that by offering his own blood no other blood would be needed to feed the spirits as he was offering the Holy Spirit as a familiar spirit to all through him—a blood sacrifice to end all blood sacrifices, according to the story, anyway.

During the American and European witch trials a notion circulated that not only did witches have familiars but also that they fed them their own blood from an odd teat.

In the late 17th century, several hundred people were tried for the crime of practicing witchcraft in Salem Village, Massachusetts.

. . . Also used as evidence were skin lesions characteristic of what were termed "devil's marks" or "witch's marks." . . . Devil's marks included a variety of skin lesions described as flat or raised, red, blue, or brown lesions, sometimes with unusual outlines. Witch's marks were most probably supernumerary nipples. It was believed that familiars (agents of the devil, usually in animal form) would receive sustenance by being suckled.[7]

In England, Elizabeth Sawyer described her witch's mark in a trial in 1621, saying, "it's a thing like a teat the bigness of the little finger and the length of half a finger which was branched at the top as a teat and it seemed as though one had sucked it."[8]

You would not be mistaken if you notice that this seems rather like a mother breastfeeding a child. In some of the witch trials the witches claimed that their familiar was one of their lost children, either miscarried or stillborn. Somehow this lost "family" member was reincarnated as an animal who was so familiar to the witch that she recognized the spirit as her lost child.

SUPERPOWERS

According to many traditions, the power of flight extended to all men in the mythical age; all could reach heaven, whether on the wings of a fabulous bird or on the clouds. . . . We have seen that the same magical powers are credited to yogins, fakirs, and alchemists. . . . "Among all things that fly the mind [manas] is the swiftest," says the Rig-Veda.

MIRCEA ELIADE,
SHAMANISM: ARCHAIC TECHNIQUES OF ECSTASY

One of the most consistent attributes gained from working with a familiar spirit is a superpower. The different types of familiar spirits through the ages gave many different superpowers. Psychic and physical abilities, prophecy, shapeshifting, astral travel, conveyance of wisdom, knowledge, and inventions are among the many abilities given to the human through the agency of the familiar. In some cases, the familiar spirit delivered special information to its receiver or to a group of people, using the receiver as a channel. Other times the familiar conveyed superhuman strength to the receiver, as was the case with the Berserkers of the Norse legends. The Berserkers were warriors who were said to take on the spirit of the bear and use its strength to aid them in becoming invincible. After taking the spirit of the bear within them and wearing the bear's skin upon their backs, they were able to perform superhuman feats of strength they would never have been able to achieve without the aid of this powerful ally.

Many of the indigenous cultures claim that familiar spirits have given them healing powers, knowledge of medicine, and instructions on how to cure diseases. These special powers will be examined in more detail in the chapters to follow.

As I delved into the research on some of the relationships involved with the familiar spirits, I found a long history of these exploits that cross into nearly every known religion. Throughout the course of history, human beings have engaged in extensive relationships with nature and with dead and nonhuman entities of all kinds to facilitate some type of exchange that often benefits human society and civilization and fosters evolution. Familiars do not only aid a single practitioner, such as a lone witch, but can also watch over much larger groups and organizations, even entire cities and countries, as a guiding intellect. Most know the use of familiars by a single individual, but it is important to recognize the larger scope of their influence over churches and spiritual practices around the globe. The United States' familiar spirit—for the colonizers, not the natives—is Lady Columbia. Often depicted with an eagle, arrows, and the flag, she was a popular figure in the 1800s and is immortalized in the huge idol known as the Statue of Liberty.

2

Shamanic Totems, the Nagual, and the Black Cat

The final level of Power that may sometimes speak or act through us, as well as communicate to us, is the inner ally or guardian spirit. Today the concept is most familiar from Native American traditions and shamanism, in which the shaman works with and may take on the persona of an animal ally in trance, but animal totems or helpers are familiar from European folktales and Norse folklore, in which the fylgia, *or "follower," appears in animal or human form. The Aztec call this the* nagual *or* tonal. *It appears in English folklore as the familiar spirit. Among the Classical Greeks, the* daemon *filled this role.*

DIANA PAXSON, *THE ESSENTIAL GUIDE TO POSSESSION,
DEPOSSESSION & DIVINE RELATIONSHIPS*

In shamanic and indigenous cultures, the idea of an animal or some other kind of spirit that you have a deep soul connection with is very commonplace. In the West, many call this a spirit animal. The term *spirit animal* is so popular in New Age and neo-shamanic culture that there are spirit animal parties that people attend like raves. The term *spirit animal* did not appear until the 1980s, according to some sources, and was not an indigenous term at all but came out of pop culture spiritualism. Even though many people have heard of a spirit animal, there are very few who might make the connection between that and the witch's familiar. The term used by many indigenous peoples is closer to *totem* and is also connected to the word *family*, much like the word witches use: *familiar*.

SHAMANIC TOTEMS AND THE NAGUAL

totem (n.) *animal or natural object considered as the emblem of a family or clan, 1760, from Algonquian (probably Ojibwa)*—doodem, *in* odoodeman *"his sibling kin, his group or family," hence, "his family mark"; also attested in French c. 1600 in form* aoutem *among the Micmacs or other Indians of Nova Scotia.* Totem pole *is 1808, in reference to west coast Canadian Indians.*

HARPER, ONLINE ETYMOLOGY DICTIONARY

The origin of the word *totem* is said to come from the Algonquian Native Americans but could be directly connected to the Mi'kmaq tribe of eastern Canada in a different form. The word *totem* is meant to infer a kind of family relation or kinship with the soul of something, and all of the totem poles, which can be found throughout North America, basically represent the familiars of each tribe in the form of a wooden statue, or idol, that declares their allegiance to their allies, which are mainly animals or spirits. Not all the creatures on totem poles are animals; some of them are supernatural beings and guardian spirits that can't be found in the animal kingdom.

My own personal experience with a totem animal, while working with Kelvin DeWolfe, a Mi'kmaq shaman, was so shocking I'm sure most of you will not believe what I'm about to tell you. I participated in a spirit journey with several others, led by DeWolfe, during which we did not eat or sleep for four days. While on the journey, I witnessed each participant's spirit animal completely cover his or her face, as if the animal face were superimposed upon the person's features like a mask. All the participants consistently saw the same animal on the same person; in other words, the animal head or visage on a particular person didn't change no matter who was seeing it. The rest of the body remained the same, which reminded me of depictions of ancient Egyptian deities with human bodies and animal heads. My teacher had an eagle head superimposed over his face; it was quite unmistakable. Needless to say, that experience forever changed how I viewed the familiar.

In South America there came to be tales of a very specific and strange kind of spirit animal and counterpart that went by the name of *nagual*. Carlos Castaneda popularized the word *nagual* almost overnight with his don Juan book series. Descriptions and depictions of the nagual are similar to what I had personally experienced, as the spirit animal is shown superimposed over the person, or worn like a suit or costume, most popularly portrayed in the *Codex Magliabechiano,* a pictorial Aztec codex dated to the mid-sixteenth century, now held in Florence, Italy.

The Mexican shamans mention the nagual as a spirit animal who plays a role as a double and an ally. The nagual is like an assistant or servant that the shaman or sorcerer uses as a source of power, such as conferring shapeshifting ability.

An "ally," [don Juan] said, is a power a man can bring into his life to help him, advise him, and give him the strength necessary to perform acts, whether big or small, right or wrong. This ally is necessary to enhance a man's life, guide his acts, and further his knowledge. In fact, an ally is the indispensable aid to knowing. Don Juan said this with great conviction and force. He seemed to choose his words carefully. He repeated the following sentence four times: "An ally will make you see and understand things about which no human being could possibly enlighten you."[1]

Nagual
Original art by Maja D'Aoust

It's difficult to trace the origins of the word *nagual*. Most scholars translate it to mean some type of sorcerer or witch. Some of the earliest references to it are in the *Codex Borgia,* a text used mostly for divination. Usually the word is like a way to knowledge or a way to know something and acquire power. Nagual is often mentioned with a sister concept known as the *tonal,* which is a reference to the human soul that the nagual is attracted to or a counterpart thereof. In *Tales of Power,* don Juan explains to Castaneda about these two aspects.

The *tonal* begins at birth and ends at death, but the *nagual* never ends. The *nagual* has no limit. I've said that the *nagual* is where power hovers. . . . For the *nagual,* there is no land, or air, or water.

. . . So the *nagual* glides, or flies, or does whatever it may do, in *nagual*'s time, and that has nothing to do with *tonal*'s time. The two things don't jibe. . . . The *tonal* and the *nagual* are two different worlds. In one you talk, in the other you act.[2]

This ally, or helper spirit, somehow becomes a connecting point between the world of spirit and the world of the living. According to Benson Saler, in his essay "Nagual, Witch and Sorcerer in a Quiché Village," it is difficult to define exactly what the entity is due to decades of misinterpretation by white Christian missionaries and European invaders. However, after extensive research in this area, Saler has determined that nagual often refers to a familiar spirit deeply connected to the individual and linked through destiny.

Among some populations, the *alter ego* is known as a person's *nagual;* among other groups, however, terms other than *nagual* are applied to it in the local vocabularies. While the *alter ego* may sometimes be a natural phenomenon, such as wind or a comet, it is most commonly reported to be an animal. Contingent on associated local beliefs, *nagual* in this sense . . . has been variously translated as "guardian spirit," "spirit-counterpart," "birth-spirit" or "birth-guardian," "soul-bearer," "companion-spirit," and "destiny animal." Subject to local variation, there are diverse methods for determining a person's *alter ego,* insofar as it is believed possible to do so; the perception of some animal, object or natural phenomenon under conditions or circumstances that are considered unusual.[3]

These types of identifications of the nagual place it as a spirit that has a specific relationship with the person and is tied to that person, providing protection or guardianship. The passage also seems to indicate that the nagual is something that can be perceived by other people, much as I saw the naguals of myself and others in the ceremony in which I participated.

Other Native American tribes describe a similar power relationship with an ally or guardian spirit that is obtained through a vision quest, which then confers supernatural abilities upon the shaman. In the Columbia River area of Oregon, the Nez Perce call it a *weyekin,* and the shaman or witches engage with it through power techniques obtained from fasting and often from sleep deprivation. The weyekin is a guardian and will protect and guide whoever is lucky enough to attract one, but attracting one takes a lot of hard work.

> To receive a weyekin, a young person around the age of 12 to 15 would go to the mountains on a vision quest. The person about to go on this quest would be tutored by a "renowned warrior, hunter, or medicine man," for boys, or for girls, "an elderly woman of reputed power." Success had much to do with how they prepared their minds. Fasting for long periods of time, going without a fire, holding their spiritual retreat in a remote and "awe inspiring" location.[4]

The accomplishment of attracting and keeping one of these allies took a lot of discipline and willpower as well as the strength to dominate it. If the person who was able to procure the spirit was unable to keep up his or her discipline, that person suffered greatly under its agency. For indigenous peoples, having access to these spirits was very practical as they were usually used to help with healing disease and working with the dead.

THE BLACK CAT AS FAMILIAR

A philosopher is a blind man in a dark room looking for a black cat that isn't there. A theologian is the man who finds it.

H. L. Mencken

The most famous animal image of the familiar in the West, at least in modern times, is undeniably the black cat. The friendship between the witch and the black cat is the basis of the majority of Halloween kitsch in the past one hundred years all over the country. American depictions of witches often show the witch with her constant companion, the dark feline. Usually, the witch and her cat are an inseparable couple. The female witch often lacks a human sexual companion, and the cat takes the place of a male soul mate, at least in the minds of some. This could be the origin of the idea of the lonely cat woman who was never married and instead prefers to express her love for a precious kitty. In American popular culture, the black cat certainly has the reputation of being a familiar spirit for witches, but this correspondence has much older roots.

> The connection of cats to women, a longstanding comparison in many cultures, has many manifestations and, in a way, parallels the connection of cats to the supernatural. The most obvious historic examples of this connection are witches and their familiars; women and cats were often burned together for crimes of witchcraft and sorcery. In fact, the cat familiar appears in one of the first "notable" Elizabethan witch trials at Chelmsford in 1566. . . . More often than not the cat was either the familiar of a witch or the witch herself transformed. It is a tenacious connection; forty years after the last official witch trial in Britain, a Bavarian nun was beheaded in 1749 for talking to her three cats, which were judged to be devils.[5]

Where did the black cat affiliation arise, and what is the connection between black cats, bad luck, and witches? Black cats used to be good luck in most of the world, especially Egypt, where they were considered patrons of the goddess Bast. Bast assumed the shape of a cat and was a symbol of immortality and longevity. Cat mummies were often buried with the pharaohs to assist them in gaining immortality.

In the second dynasty in Egypt, almost every household had a black cat. Black cats were considered to be the luckiest because of their friendship with Bast. This situation changed when the Roman

Bast, Egyptian cat goddess
Original art by Maja D'Aoust

emperor Theodosius I, who ruled from 379 to 395 CE, began enforcing Christianity in Alexandria and then all over Egypt and into Europe. The Christian church began to make it illegal to practice pagan religions. The pagans were murdered in the millions; often death was the punishment for being caught participating in pagan practices. Since the majority of Egyptians at the time owned a black cat, the cat became a convenient way to identify Egyptians with pagan beliefs. Emperor Theodosius issued a decree that idolatry and the worship of household guardian spirits was strictly forbidden. Most families kept statues of Bast and pet cats as a way of worshipping her idol, so the affiliation between black cats and paganism became inseparable.[6] Anyone caught with a black cat was promptly murdered for being a heretic in the eyes of the Christian lord. This eradication of paganism was so thorough that no one knew how to speak the language or read hieroglyphs until the discovery of the Rosetta stone more than a thousand years later.

Years later, about 1233, Pope Gregory IX issued a papal bull called *Vox in Rama*, which declared that black cats were demonic and carried satanic forces. It was a completely fantastical story of a Luciferian figure who was a hybrid feline that talked to a black cat familiar spirit. In a further effort to eradicate paganism, black cats all across Europe were killed as a result of this ignorance and having them around became unlucky.

Witch with feline familiar
Original art by Maja D'Aoust

In the witch trials in America, a woman caught with a cat was identified as a witch in a weird echo through time and space of the Egyptian cat persecutions and European follies.

> *My wife, who at heart was not a little tinctured with superstition, made frequent allusion to the ancient popular notion, which regarded all black cats as witches in disguise.*
>
> EDGAR ALLAN POE, "THE BLACK CAT"

3

The Fetch, the Libido, the Celibate, and the Familiar

Loving relationships with spiritual beings can be the most joyous, pleasurable and rewarding experience in life. There is nothing inherently dangerous, or perverse, or evil, about sex with a spirit. Just the opposite. A study of historical accounts and ancient legends, as well as years of personal interaction with spirits, have led me to conclude that loving and erotic unions with angels and lesser beings such as elementals are a precious gift that should be cherished with the highest feelings of respect and gratitude by those who are fortunate enough to enjoy them. The crucial feature of these relationships is love.

DONALD TYSON, *SEXUAL ALCHEMY*

When examining histories of topics considered taboo, one finds many aspects of sexuality but perhaps none as shunned as the idea of supernatural sexual relationships. Most of these relationships were considered to be Witches' Sabbath practices of communion with the devil. Humans engaging with spirits for carnal purposes was prosecutable for hundreds of years during the witch trials. Unraveling the mystery of these strange practices can be formidable due to censorship and judgments, but upon closer inspection, human–spirit sexual relationships permeate the majority of our religions and mythologies.

LIBIDO, DESIRE, AND THE ANIMAL NATURE

Where does Eros end? Where does magic begin? The answer seems very simple: at the very moment Eros is made manifest, so is magic also. That is why erotic magic, at bottom, represents the starting point of all magic.

IOAN P. COULIANO,
EROS AND MAGIC IN THE RENAISSANCE

Another word that came to be affiliated with the concept of the witch's familiar is the term *fetch*. The fetch was specifically the animal sexual nature of the witch, and it had a magnetic and attractive attribute to it. The fetch was very popular as a character throughout Europe and was long affiliated with European witches. The history of this term is where we get the word *fetching* to describe someone as being attractive. The term *fetch* was affiliated with the image of the person, like an apparition, which is sometimes called a wraith. The word has a long history in Europe, especially Irish and Celtic fairy faith locations, and there is usage of it dating back to 1787 in Francis Grose's book on paranormal phenomenon, *Superstitions: Omens, Charms, Cures.*

The fetch was described in many instances as something that could really work in the physical world and make appearances depending on how strong the desire that formed it was. The fetch was like a concentration of desire and thus had a powerful magnetic force affiliated with it that could draw things to it, much like a magnet.

The fetch was the mechanism through which the witch accomplished her spell and was responsible for manifesting her wish. Many felt that this was done purely through a kind of phantasmagoria of the

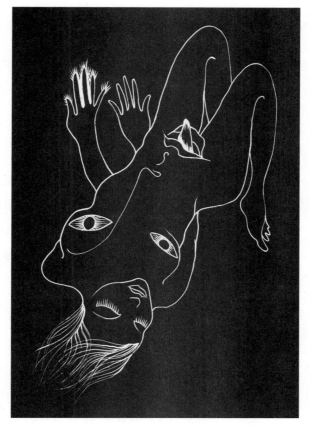

Reclining witch
Original art by Maja D'Aoust

imagination. For example, repeating a sexual fantasy of a certain person whom the witch desired would, over time, imbue the fetch with the ability to attract that person to the witch. Whatever this mysterious force is that drives us together in our relationships is the same that drives together subatomic particles to make matter and energy, sodium and chloride to make salt, and clumps of matter to make new galaxies. Your mother and father were driven together by the same force that creates sulfuric acid. Whatever this force may be, it is the driving force of the entire universe; we all fall under its sway. Spirits, too, fall under its sway to join with us. Desire drives us all like a team of horses.

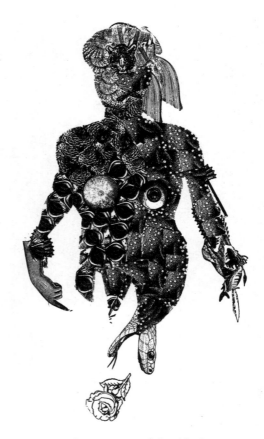

The mystery of the libido
Original art by Jon Graham

Phantasm is a wonderful word that has gone out of vogue. A phantasm is a figment of the imagination or an illusion and is related to the word *fantasy,* the faculty or activity of imagining things. Both words come from the Greek *phantasma* or *phantazein,* which means "to make visible" or "to show." The root word *bha* means "to shine." A phantasm can be made by projecting an image in the light—like a trick of the light that appears almost as a mirage. The image can also be projected in our mind's eye. This is how we "see" things when we imagine them, like a daydream.

When there is an object of your love and desire, you take in his or her image through your eyes. That image enters your brain, and you fix-ate on it, obsessively sometimes. Through the fascination of your fantasy, you transform the person you have fallen in love with into a phantasm, a phantom. The phantasm is your ideal, not the real person. You create an imaginational double of a person through the action of fantasy.

This concept is discussed at length in the book *The Anatomy of Melancholy* by Robert Burton, in which the melancholic state of depress-ives is partially attributed to an excess of these types of fantasies. The connection between these kinds of obsessive imagination fantasies and sexual health and dysfunction was examined by psychiatrist Richard von Krafft-Ebing in the foundational work *Psychopathia Sexualis*. Sigmund Freud later expounded upon the relationship between phantasms and the libido as an imagination-driven aspect of the self.

Such is its character, fundamentally unchangeable. The ideas which the libido now takes over in order to hold its energy belong to the system of the unconscious, and are therefore subject to its peculiar processes, especially elaboration and displacement. Conditions are set up here which are entirely comparable to those of dream forma-tion. Just as the latent dream, the fulfillment of a wish-phantasy, is first built up in the unconsciousness, but must then pass through conscious processes before, censored and approved, it can enter into the compromise construction of the manifest dream, so the ideas representing the libido in the unconscious must still contend against the power of the fore-conscious ego. The opposition that has arisen against it in the ego follows it down by a "counter-siege" and forces it to choose such an expression as will serve at the same time to express itself. Thus, then, the symptom comes into being as a much distorted offshoot from the unconscious libidinous wish-fulfillment, an artificially selected ambiguity.[1]

The word *fascinate* comes from the Latin verb *fascinare* or *fascinum,* meaning "spell, witchcraft," so to fascinate is to put someone under a spell or bewitch. We are fascinated by things that draw our attention, like a twinkling light we cannot look away from. Sexual fantasies tend to have an obsessive nature and an ability to attract; this is what most sex magic draws upon.

The word *fairy* is directly related to the word *fate: fate* comes from the Latin *fatum,* meaning "that which has been spoken," from the root *bha,* and refers to words spoken from the gods themselves, as in fated or ordained and related to destiny.[2] *Fairy* is derived from *fata,* "the fates," the plural of *fatum,* with its connection to the three Fates of Greek mythology and the goddess of fate. Fairies were known to have the power of fascination and enchantment over people and could influence them through their libidinous attachments. Historically, the idea of "fame and fortune" is connected to visualization and wishes sent to the fairies, gods, and Fates, the guardians of our destiny. The goddess Fortuna was perhaps the most famous familiar spirit who embodied this concept. *Fame* has the same root as *fate, bha,* "to speak," and suggests being spoken about, rather like gossip. The fairies in many occult references were said to guide our destiny, fame, and fortune with spells of spoken words and enchantments.

From the word *phantom* also arises the word *phantasmagoria,* which is an exhibition of optical effects and illusions. In the late eighteenth century, a phantasmagoria was a kind of horror theater that used magic lanterns. These lanterns used light to project an image on a screen or even into the audience, much like how fantasies are projected from the eye to our minds. Prestidigitation magicians used magic lanterns in their staged séances and conjurations of the dead. The first time audiences saw these phantom images, they thought the spirits of the dead had been raised. The magic lantern eventually evolved into modern cinema.

The fetch is the primary fantasy operator, upon which we project our phantasmagoria of desires, whether known or unknown, conscious or subconscious. The fetch acts as an assistant or servant, much in the "familiar" way earlier described. This entity fulfills the wishes of the witch, much like a genie, or like the wish-seeking libido mentioned by Freud, and accomplishes this through the attractive power of love. In *Eros and Magic in the Renaissance,* Ioan Couliano writes:

> The fundamental idea of the treatise is that "love rules the world," that "the strongest chain is that of Venus" [Giordano Bruno, *De vinculis in genere*, 696]. Eros "is the Lord of the world: he pushes, directs, controls and appeases everyone. All other bonds are reduced to that one, as we see in the animal kingdom where no female and no male tolerates rivals, even forgetting to eat and drink, even at the risk of life itself." . . . "Indeed the chain of chains is love" [ibid.].[3]

In the case of using the sexual energy of a witch or person to attract a familiar spirit, there are practices that have long been used for that aim. The libido, when purposefully withdrawn from the world and focused entirely on a spirit, can make strange things happen. The techniques used to control, repress, or sublimate the human sex drive are discussed at great length in many religious and philosophical texts. The practice of celibacy to achieve spiritual powers is well known. A not uncommon belief is that by disengaging with our sexual animal natures we can achieve a more elevated spiritual nature. In some Christian churches celibacy is practiced to achieve virtue and piousness and attract the Holy Spirit. Islam and Judaism do not seem to promote celibacy and instead venerate marriage, extolling its ability to obtain spiritual graces. In Judaism, some consider it a sin against God to engage in celibacy because you are not using the life-giving gifts of your body to be fruitful and multiply.

When the libido cannot find a desirable human, it can be drawn into fantastical imaginary pursuits, longing for an idealized lover who exists only in the imagination. The sexual fantasies of an unsatisfied libido can also attract nonhuman spirits, and perhaps not even consciously. Restraining the libido from seeking human lovers can attract other forms of soul mates, such as the familiar spirits referenced earlier.

In *Psychological Anthropology Reconsidered,* John Ingham, a noted authority in the field of psychology, makes the following observation.

> According to Freud, sublimation begins with the withdrawal of object libido into the self. As the libido is withdrawn from objects and reinvested in the ego, it becomes narcissistic libido, neutralized energy or desexualized libido. . . . This neutralized libido can then energize the pursuit of social status or attachments to persons, cultural artifacts, or supernatural beings. Sublimation can tap emotionally colored preoedipal and oedipal object-relations schemas or object- and power-seeking libido in a broad sense. . . . Power-seeking libido can merge with aggressive energy and destructive impulses, which are also subject to modulation and sublimation. "The instinct of destruction moderated and tamed and as it were inhibited in its aim, must, when it is directed towards objects, provide the ego with the satisfaction of its vital needs and with control over nature."[4]

There are many things that the libido can be focused upon, in phantasmagoria, and often the nature of the focus will be what draws in the specific familiar spirit.

When the libido is thrown onto an object, activity, or body part, instead of on a supernatural or human lover, this is called fetishism. Appropriately enough nowadays the term *fetish* refers to an object that is not usually thought to be sexual, such as a shoe. It can also mean an inanimate object worshipped for its magical powers or because it is believed to be inhabited by a spirit, which constitutes the practice of idolatry and idol worship. We can observe just this type of idol worship in Christian churches scattered around the globe as supplicants bow and pray to statues of Christ on the cross, imbuing these objects with their sincere affections. Ironically, the very religion that forbade the pagans from praying to statues of their gods merely replaced those statues with the stone and wooden visages of Christ, Mary, and the Catholic saints. The practice of idolatry is most memorably denounced in the story of

The ritual object of the idol
Original art by Jon Graham

Moses and the golden calf. When Moses descended from heaven with the sapphire tablets, he became so depressed because his people were practicing idolatry instead of listening to him that he crushed the word of God upon his knee to punish them.

Some tales of idol worship involve the idol coming to life or taking on real characteristics. An African trickster god or god of the crossroads called Elegua or Esu-Elgebara is worshipped in the Yoruba religion, and many believers have statues of him, which they claim speak to them and sometimes even move.

Unlike cowry shells, charms, animal entrails and so on, spirits and "fetishes" are essentially "personalized"; they are represented as being able to speak and act in some degree like people. Thus, the *nyakarondo* Mijago could and did sing and dance, and both it and Igondo could move from place to place without human aid. So, as well as divining, these powers are thought to be able to act as familiars to their masters, and to carry out their bidding. . . . Indeed they are thought to be so powerful as to be dangerous to their owners as well as to those against whom he may send them. I was told that a man who owns a Nyakaraondo cannot get rid of it or chase it away even if he wants to do so. . . . Such powerful fetishes may indicate to its owner through dreams that they require some living thing such as a chicken, a goat, or even, it is said, a human being, to be made over to them by sacrifice and if they do not get what they want they may kill their masters and their whole families.[5]

In the story of Pygmalion from Ovid's *Metamorphoses,* a sculptor falls in love with a statue he created as an ideal lover. Pygmalion focuses his adoration so intensely on the statue that his phantasmagoria comes to life and engages in conversation with him. In Egypt, too, there were tales of statues coming to life, and in the Jewish tradition there were stories of the golems, which were men made of mud and stone that the Jewish rabbis could bring to life with magic. Fantastical as these stories and myths are, their worldwide occurrence indicates that people have been having these fantasies for quite some time.

THE CELIBATE AND THE FAMILIAR

In spite of the changes in political life, in spite of the opulence and magnificence of the palmy days of Rome, the cult of Vesta stood unchanging for a thousand years.

SIR T. C. WORSFOLD, *THE HISTORY OF THE VESTAL VIRGINS OF ROME*

There is a strange thing that many, though not all, of the witches and individuals who acquire a familiar seem to have in common: they stop having sex. The story of the spinster who lives alone, unmarried, with lots of cats is the epitome of this stereotype, but upon closer examination there seems to be a direct connection between the libido and the familiar spirit in many instances.

Those who are able to channel and receive a spirit stop engaging in physical sexual acts in favor of intercourse with the familiar spirit from whom they are receiving the prophecies. Isolation, little human contact, and a kind of monastic hermitage are all key ingredients in the taking on of a familiar spirit in this way. The shamans who engage in this practice tend to live alone on the outskirts of villages. The priests of the Druids were said to follow these practices and worked closely with animals and nature spirits while remaining celibate.

Druid
Original art by Maja D'Aoust

Spending time grieving the dead as a widow, alone at cemeteries, is a common thread in the experience of acquiring a familiar spirit as well. In many cultures the familiar spirits have connotations with graveyards, dead ancestors, and family lineages. Women who have lost loved ones and attend to their graves may have a higher probability of contacting a familiar spirit.

Being alone, not having sex, and connecting to the dead seem to provide ideal circumstances for an individual to attract an imaginary friend or spirit who then may stream information through the human host or conduit.

Christians practiced this ancient technique, for which the witches were ridiculed. There are detailed accounts of an early Christian scholar and ascetic who imposed celibacy on himself through the drastic measure of self-castration. Known simply by the name Origen, he studied the New Testament and wrote commentaries on the Gospel of John, Genesis, and Psalms, among others, and wrote books on the Resurrection of Jesus and the ten books of Stromata, as well as extensive work on the Old Testament. Origen used his celibacy to channel a muse to assist him in his studies and writing. The results can be seen in his prolific works, and this channeling may account for the prodigious amount of information he produced: he was receiving it from a spirit mentor. The Bible was, therefore, mostly received and prepared through the familiar spirit of a self-castrated oracle.

There was some controversy over whether Origen was a pagan and a heretic because of his extreme practices and his place of birth. Born and raised in Egypt, his name meant "born from Horus," an obvious Egyptian pagan reference. Sigmund Freud noted the connection between Origen's work and his libido, as Thomas Hywel Hughes states in his book.

He [Freud] speaks of Origen's conversion in just this way. The original type of his nature was extravert and the tendency strongly sexual, but this is reversed, and he suppresses his sexual tendencies and becomes a brooder and seer. So the original type is reversed, and this is his conversion. "It is then the process of breaking the natural instinctive course, and a transition to another attitude." How does this come about? What is the motive power? The motive power appears to be the fact that the over-development of one type or of one instinct in a certain direction tends, by a purely natural process of the mind, to compensation in another. If we seek further into the question of this tendency, Jung suggests that in the case of the over-developed instinct or instincts, there is a heaping up of energy. The libido of that instinct is not all used up, as it were, in the activity of the instinct itself. There is an overplus of energy, and this overflows into channels hitherto not consciously used.[6]

The vestal virgins of Rome were one of the most celebrated and possibly one of the longest-running religious orders, lasting for a little more than a thousand years. These priestesses of Vesta, goddess of the hearth, were diviners employed by the state of Rome and practiced celibacy so as to receive prophecies from spirits and gods. They had to give up sexual relationships with mortal men and forgo marriage to form relationships with familiars who would provide them with supernatural and psychic abilities. The recorded accurate predictions of the vestals were many and uncanny, but they were also off sometimes (they were only human after all), which called into question the efficacy of divination in general.

For the Romans, this was a sacred institution, and divination by way of restraining the libido to attract a spirit was well understood and respected. The vestals were given money from the government to perform their services and regarded as valuable and indispensable. Unlike the later Christian church, which saw fortune-telling as the work of Satan, the divination practices of these witches through the spirits were among the most holy activities in which a woman could engage.

The vestals took their cues and practices from an even older tradition that many believe the Romans stole from the Greeks and Turks, which is quite possible since the Romans stole and appropriated all manner of things unapologetically. The Greeks had for many years prior adopted the practice of engaging virgin oracles, often called witches but also known as priestesses. Practices of celibacy among the oracles for communion with spirits are well known, as discussed by lecturer in Classical studies Sue Blundell.

> Two prominent instances of priestesses assigned to male deities occurred at Dodona and Delphi, oracular shrines where answers to queries addressed to a god were transmitted via a female agent. In both of these sanctuaries the priestesses were non-fertile and celibate. Although lifelong celibacy was not a condition commonly imposed by Greek religion as a temporary state, it seems to have been considered important when a human female was called upon to act as the mouthpiece for a god. As a woman, the priestess was available for entry by a male deity; as a woman who had no sexual relations with mortal man, she was reserving herself for the god alone.[7]

4

Greek Belly-Talkers, Witches, Sibyls, and Priestesses

O long-silent Sybil,
you of the winged dreams,
Speak out from your temple of light

LAWRENCE FERLINGHETTI,
"TO THE ORACLE AT DELPHI"

The use of familiar spirits extended all over Greece and surrounding areas of modern-day Turkey. These ancient traditions—which served unique purposes and provided much insight into all manner of activities, from prophecy to government—are very important to exploring relationships between humans and spirits.

GREEK BELLY-TALKERS AND THE SIBYLS

The Oracle of Delphi: The Pythia is important because she stands on the thresholds of the pagan and the Christian worlds. She is meant to stand as the image of an inheritance from or throwback to foul, forgotten, chthonic beginnings: she provides the vent or doorway through which the dark, demonic, imperfectly superseded world of magic may creep back.

STEVEN CONNOR, *DUMBSTRUCK*

One of the most famous passages in the Bible about witches using familiar spirits is found in the Book of Samuel and relates the story of the Witch of Endor. In this tale, King Saul is warned not to consult any women with familiar spirits, or soothsayers, regarding the outcome of an impending battle he was to engage in but rather to trust in God that he would be victorious. There was only one form of divination thought appropriate to consult at the time: the Urim and the Thummim, which were two sacred stones held in a breast plate worn by a priest.

Saul chose not to seek this divination, but he fell into anxiety and fear and, ashamed of himself, decided to consult the Witch of Endor. He entreated her to call upon the spirit of a dead patriarch and seek its counsel and wisdom so that he would be able to go forward in confidence. The witch predicted, counter to what God had said, that he would die in the battle, and sure enough, that is what happened. Many Christians and Jews say this happened because Saul believed the witch and did not trust God.

I feel the true meaning of this tale was lost somewhere in the annals of history. The story examines how humans deal with anxiety and fear when approaching a difficult situation and whom they choose to listen to for advice. When we hand over our power to anything other than our own capabilities, we begin to unravel; regardless of the prophecies foretold by any oracle, the truth should be found in our own sincerity. To me the tale of the Witch of Endor was not about her prediction but about Saul's inappropriate fixation on outcome. Funny how Saul's insecurities become projected upon the witch, who fulfills the role of scapegoat. Many people misuse divination, in my opinion, and seek outcome-oriented advice, when they should be focused on inner truth and growth. Maybe some of the taboos surrounding these interactions were intended to warn people about the proper use of divination.

The purpose of the divination and of the daimon, or ally, is for nothing other than to test the sincerity of your own heart. You are not meant to believe or disbelieve any fate decreed by any oracle. Rather, it is something for your heart to go up against, like a sounding board or a test of faith, so that you can discover or confirm what your heart already knows, deep within, to be true. This may seem confusing, but this is a hidden truth within all oracles and divination systems, which have among their archetypes the core of your own heart. After circling around something for long enough with the vultures of your mind, it is certain that you will arrive there sooner or later if you follow the spiral to the end inside your heart. In the most ancient versions of stories of familiar spirits, we are similarly instructed not to blindly listen and follow them but instead to form a relationship with the spirits, which helps us establish, with their guidance, our own inner compass. Angels can give us instructions, but they do not think and feel for us. To have a proper relationship with a familiar is not codependent—as if you would ask your mate what to eat for dinner instead of feeling your own hunger—but is two independent forms of sentience that coexist together, informing each other without losing sovereignty.

In the story, the Witch of Endor has a familiar spirit, but Saul does not want to talk to that spirit; he wants her to resurrect the soul of the deceased patriarch Samuel and ask for his insight or information. According to Jewish sources, the witch did not want to do this because King Saul himself had passed a law forbidding such a resurrection, so she feared for her life, but Saul told her to just do it anyway and assured her that she would not get in trouble. Seems there is a long history of lawmakers making exceptions for themselves when they wish to do something illegal. The rabbis used a parable to explain this action on Saul's part, as explained by Tamar Kadari in her article "Necromancer of Endor: Midrash and Aggadah."

> The Rabbis illustrate the monarch's inconsistency by means of a parable: a king entered a certain land, and ordered that all the roosters in the land were to be slaughtered that night. When he wanted to set forth, he asked: "Is there no cock to crow?" His servants told him: "It was you who ordered that they be slaughtered!" (*Lev. Rabbah* 26:7). Saul Lieberman observes that this parable

depicts the Roman custom of augury with roosters before setting out to battle. On the basis of how the roosters ate their food, the Romans divined whether they would return victorious or not. This parable exemplified Saul's sorry condition. He presents himself as the executor of the divine mandate to remove the necromancers and soothsayers, but immediately following this he is revealed before his servants in all his shame, when he himself consults a necromancer. The necromancer is compared to the augur's rooster, which was one of the means employed when confronted with uncertainty of the future.[1]

This watching of the birds is a form of divination and oracle still practiced by the Catholic Church under the sanction of God, unlike the divination done by witches, which is taboo. In the tale of the Witch of Endor we see a pagan practitioner who uses familiar spirits to gain the superpower of prophecy. She is at first reviled but then sought out by those who decreed her to be evil. It would appear at the end of the day that the witch was efficacious in her work and provided all that was asked of her regardless of the judgments upon her uncleanliness.

The Witch of Endor is only one example of a much larger tradition of these types of oracles extending far and wide but made popular in Greece. There is a vast history of the practice of consulting a familiar spirit and the dead for purposes of obtaining information, or sometimes, it just happens spontaneously.

A peculiar Greek word used in the Septuagint version of the Bible to describe the Witch of Endor sheds some light on the practices of the witch and her familiar spirit in history. The word *engastrimythoi* was long ago removed from the vocabulary of these discussions. It means "belly-talker" (*gastri* is "belly," and *myth* means "speech"), or one who speaks from his belly, although some seem to think that it is not the belly but the womb. This distinction is mentioned by sixteenth-century courtier and poet Guillaume de Saluste Du Bartas: "So all incest, the pale engastromith / Rul'd by the furious spirit he's haunted with, / Speakes in his womb."[2]

The word *ventriloquist* is another version of "belly-talker" (from the Latin *ventral* meaning "belly" and *loqui,* "talk"). *Ventriloquist* was later appropriated by the entertainment industry, but originally it was meant to convey that the oracles did not speak, but rather, the spirit within them spoke.

Engastrimythos (ἐγγαστρίμυθος, lit. "belly-talker"), a witchlike descendant of the ancient Sibyls or prophetesses. *Engastrimythoi,* often male, were ventriloquists who disguised their voices and made mantic utterances, as if a deity or demon were acting within and speaking through them.[3]

This strange word possibly means that the dead used the oracle like a modern ventriloquist uses his dummy, possessing the oracle and speaking through her. This would make the witch's role in things more like a puppet. Some stories seemed to also indicate that the oracles could speak to someone without actually talking, like telepathy: the voice of the oracle could be heard in the head of the querent without the belly-talker's lips moving. A similar thing happens in the film *The Lord of the Rings* when the elf queen Galadriel speaks to all of the fellowship with her mind by getting in their heads. Like a ventriloquist who throws his voice into a dummy, the belly-talker oracles could throw their voices into the minds of the querents.

There are many, especially Christians, who have denounced this method of prophecy as false and have sometimes made fun of it. Some said that the person performing these divinatory rites took a demon within him to intentionally give a false prophecy so as to trick people, others thought that it was involuntary demonic possession, and still others stated that it was all made up. After the spiritualist movement occurred in Europe and America, many mediums were debunked as fakers, as popular opinion turned against these ancient ways and the practices were largely abandoned. Despite the relatively new debunking of this tradition, it has lasted thousands of years, and hundreds of thousands of people have traversed the globe for the sole purpose of seeking counsel with a belly-talker, or belly-myther. Rowan A. Greer and Margaret M. Mitchell, in their book examining the story of Saul and the Witch of Endor, discuss the origin of this term.

> Like "belly-myther" [ἐγγαστρίμυθος], is a *foreign* term and a *negative* term, which for Christian (and Jewish) readers was associated with pagan, and especially *Greek,* divinatory practices. The practices done by ἐγγαστρίμυθος are expressly forbidden by God elsewhere in the Bible in laws addressed to Israel and appropriated by Christians. . . . The Septuagintal translator had transferred a somewhat mysterious reference to ancient Mesopotamian-styled mantics into a stereotypical Greek form of alien prophetic speech.[4]

The term *belly-talker* was used not only for the Witch of Endor but also to describe an ancient tradition of many oracles who came to be known as the sibyls. One of the most well-known members of this tradition and lineage was the Oracle of Delphi, who, through consultations with familiar spirits, delivered oracles—prophecies and advice. The tradition of the sibyls extends back to an unknown point in human history, as we only have access to what is recorded, but based on some cave paintings that depict goddesses affiliated with this practice it would appear to have its roots in prehistory.

THE LOST PRIESTESSES

The lord whose is the oracle at Delphi neither utters nor hides his meaning, but shows it by a sign. . . . The Sibyl, with raving lips uttering things mirthless, unbedizened, and unperfumed, reaches over a thousand years with her voice, thanks to the god in her.

HERACLITUS

The sibyl oracles were remarkably famous and well reputed and found scattered all over Europe. Most of the sibyls were said to have come from the East, which will be explained in a tale of Abraham shortly. The word *sibyl* is highly disputed as to its origins and etymology. Some say it is derived from the goddess Cybele, and both *sibyl* and the name of the goddess have the same meaning, "cave dweller," as most of the oracles, like the Oracle of Delphi, performed their functions in caves. *Sibyl* comes from the Latin *sibylla,* which some suggest was derived from the Greek word *theobule,* meaning "divine will or counsel." Most translations state that the word means "mouth of God." According to the *Jewish Encyclopedia* the word may have originated in early Semitic Babylon, and it has also been translated as "Ancient of God," which conveys both the association of the sibyl with old age and its spiritual focus.

Libyan sibyl
Engraving by Baccio Baldini, British Museum (ca. 1470–1480)

The priestesses of The Great Pagan Goddess Cybele (Kybele—cave dweller) would, through a transformation by the Greeks, be confused with and eventually known as the Sibyls. The Great Goddess of Asia Minor is the oldest true Goddess known, predating the Goddesses of the Sumerian and Egyptians by at least 5,000 years. While there have been Goddess figurines found which date to 30,000 years ago, they come to us without knowledge of their origin or character of the Goddess they represent. A figurine found at Çatal Hüyük, dating to 8,000 years ago, depicts the Mother Goddess squatting in the process of giving birth while flanked by two leopards. In later centuries, the leopards would be changed to lions—the metamorphosed Atalanta and Hippomenes, though leopards, were considered to be female lions by the ancients. Her worship was originally combined with that of the Bull of Heaven, which is also prominently displayed at Çatal Hüyük.

A transformation of sounds, which may well have been Sybele that early in history, appears two thousand years later in Sumer as Siburi, the Divine Barmaid who held the keys to descent into the underworld. She was in fact the earthly Priestess of the Sumerian Goddess Inanna, holding the keys "Me" of the Holy Tavern and Cult Harlotry—though a Harlot was actually a priestess of the Egyptian Goddess Hathor.[5]

In ancient Greek and Roman depictions of her, Cybele is always shown holding keys, a symbol later appropriated by the pope. All over the Vatican can be seen the shield with the two crossed keys that were once held in the hand of the goddess.

Although today we mostly know male gods, there was a time when goddesses reigned supreme. The most powerful of these goddesses were the earth goddesses, also known as the dark mothers, who held the power of creation and destruction. These deities were venerated and feared. They were known by many names in many cultures, such as Kali and Demeter, but the key figure we shall be focusing on in this book is the goddess Cybele. She was a component in many of the predominant religions that we know today, and yet very few people within mainstream religions such as Christianity and Judaism have ever heard her name.

The name Cybele is steeped in mystery and has several meanings, in addition to "cave dweller" as mentioned earlier. Originally stemming from Kybele, and possibly Kybaba or Kubaba, this name is popularly interpreted to mean "Mountain Mother." In Rome, Cybele was known as Magna Mater, which means "Great Mother." In ancient Sumeria the name Kubaba was given to a supposedly real woman who was the only female to be listed with the kings. Cybele was known for her rulership over animals, fortresses, and walls; she was a fertility goddess and so was sometimes depicted giving birth. She was usually accompanied by lions or large cats and hawks or other birds of prey.

Statue of Cybele with her two guardian lions
Engraving by Bernard de Montfaucon, from Montfaucon, *Antiquity Explained,
and Represented in Sculptures,* translated by David Humphreys
(London: J. Tonson and J. Watts, 1721–1725)

Cybele was a popular Roman deity and appeared in many temples around Rome. Her vast empire spread throughout Europe and Asia. Most scholars say that she originated in Anatolia, now known as Turkey. According to most scholars, Cybele's point of origin is Mount Ida, in northwestern Turkey. Many remains of statues and temples of Cybele have been found in Turkey. Her stronghold was very close to Istanbul, or Constantinople, near the ancient city of Troy.

The origin of Vatican City is steeped in the history of the goddess Cybele. The wall enclosing the Vatican mirrors Cybele's mural crown, which represents city walls. St. Peter's Basilica is built on top of a temple or shrine to Cybele. The Roman emperor Constantine took over the grounds and ordered the building of the basilica, robbing the goddess's followers of a place of worship and diminishing her glory. Originally in that location was a Phrygian temple and grave mound.

THE METEORITE

Go and catch a falling star,
Get with child a mandrake root,
Tell me where all past years are,
Or who cleft the devil's foot,
Teach me to hear mermaids singing,
Or to keep off envy's stinging,
And find
What wind
Serves to advance an honest mind.

JOHN DONNE, "SONG: GO AND
CATCH A FALLING STAR"

The story of the secret identity of Cybele is far more fascinating than the myths and stories surrounding this Mother Goddess who was noteworthy for her priests who publicly castrated themselves in ritual ceremonies. Her true nature can be found in her origins at Mount Ida.

According to the legends, one day a massive meteorite fell to Earth and landed on top of the mountain. The locals named this meteorite Cybele: she was no lady at all but a large black stone, by some accounts sixteen feet long. Some say that her name, interpreted by some to mean "Mountain Mother," was meant to reflect her birth on top of the mountain. This makes Cybele an *idol* in the most classical sense. She was a living stone that was adored and prayed to by thousands of humans. With so many libidos intensely focused on this object, it could be true that the meteorite had mind-altering attributes, or perhaps its power was due to the electromagnetic properties of the meteor.

It was a fairly common practice to worship meteorites in ancient times, which is not difficult to believe considering how spectacular and amazing the event of a meteorite landing would be. Cybele was just one example of a meteorite enshrined in a temple; she certainly was not the first. There was a long tradition of keeping these types of stones in temples. Called Baetylus, these sacred stones were considered to be alive and endowed with spirits, just like the idol stone of Elegua in Africa. A famous stone known as Zeus was thought to have been eaten by Chronos; kept at the temple at Delphi, it was delicately cared for by the temple priestesses.

Around 204 BCE, the Romans brought Cybele, as represented by the meteorite, to Rome. At the time Hannibal, the Carthaginian general, was threatening Rome. The Sibylline Books of prophecy predicted that Cybele would free Italy from this scourge. Shortly after the stone was brought to Rome, Hannibal and his army left. The stone was housed in a temple on the Palatine Hill honoring the goddess of victory. The temple was soon thereafter rededicated to Cybele, becoming the first temple in Rome to honor her. A number of temples were built in Rome honoring Cybele, including one on Vatican Hill.

In 380 CE, some sixty years after Emperor Constantine had St. Peter's Basilica built on Vatican Hill, Christianity became the official religion of the Roman Empire, by order of Emperor Theodosius. Romulus Augustus, reigning from 475 to 476 CE, is considered the last emperor of the Western Roman Empire. It was about this time, according to the literature, that the Cybele meteorite disappeared from the Palatine. The last documented sighting of it was in about 300 CE, and it likely didn't survive the sack of Rome by the Goths in 410 CE. Someone stole the giant meteorite, and from there her whereabouts are a mystery.

There is another rather conspiratorial theory of what became of Cybele that no doubt will arouse some debate and disagreement, but the consideration of the correspondences provides some insight. It turns out that the major figure in the worship of Islam is also a black stone, housed at the temple known as the Kaaba. I find the name Kaaba of interest because it is similar to Kubaba, one of Cybele's names. The word *kaaba* means "cube," while in many of the Roman depictions of Cybele, or Kubaba, she is shown with a four-walled square fortress on top of her head, forming a cube. There could be at least an etymological connection here if nothing else.

The meteorite currently held in the Kaaba shows up in 600 CE—one hundred years after Cybele disappears from Rome. It stands to reason that the stone in the Kaaba could quite possibly be a fragment of the Cybele meteorite. The Kaaba stone is said to have been discovered by Mohammed himself. It is the very stone that he claims carried him into heaven, where he received the word of God.

Consequently, this meteorite became the center of worship of Islam. The Kaaba is a pilgrimage site where thousands of people have an ecstatic experience as they swirl around the shiny black meteorite. This practice is quite similar to the worship of Cybele in Turkey, where her followers go into altered states. People literally die every year, many of them trampled in attempts to get close to this black and shiny stone idol. This could be viewed as idolatry in its most classic pagan form. Although officially it is held that the worship is focused on Allah rather than the stone in the Kaaba, the fact that people are willing to give up their lives to this stone is an indication of how much value it holds for them in their beliefs.

So essentially, regardless of the possible connections to Cybele directly, it is undeniable that we have the Catholic Church arising around the same time that a stone idol is brought to Rome; we find Catholic sites with Black Madonna statues made of stone, believed by some to be idols made from meteorites; we have Islam and the pilgrimage to a black stone as one of the religion's core pillars; and we have the pagans worshipping stone idols. It's an interesting phenomenon that there should be odd meteorites all over the place where large religious institutions arose. But perhaps it's not so mysterious that fallen stars would have an affiliation with heaven for the world's religions. Stone idols that represent familiar spirits have a strong pull throughout history, which deserves further examination, even if the only power they contain is placed upon them by the human imagination.

Artemis of Ephesus
Anonymous eighteenth-century engraving

To return to the sibyl oracles and their familiars, it seemed they preferred to be contained within a stone cave and then attract a spirit into their living bodies to deliver their prophecies. The Oracle of Delphi in Greece was considered to have a very powerful familiar spirit. The first recorded oracle at Delphi had a dragon as her familiar spirit, and a fierce one at that. This dragon was thought to give the oracle her prophecies, powers, and wisdom and act as her fierce guardian and protector. The name of this dragon was Python, and from here we get the word for a large nonvenomous snake. The cave the oracle divined in came to be known as the Pythia, in her guardian's honor, and the high priestess was also called Pythia. This cave was also compared to a womb and represented the Earth Goddess herself, who provides our home in both birth and death. The Pythia cave provided an entrance into the Earth Goddess so that supplicants could partake of her wisdom. There may be a further connection to *pithos,* the Greek name for a large storage container. *Pithoi* (plural) were used as burial urns or coffins to inter the bones of the deceased, as well as to store grains and liquids. The ancient Egyptians also used covered urns, called canopic jars, to store the viscera of the dead.

Some believe that the familiar spirits are mostly within the Earth, or chthonic. Because of their association with ancestors or dead spirits, and therefore with graveyards, it makes sense that they would originate underground or in the underworld. Somehow, the Oracle of Delphi in her cave inside the Earth was placing herself in the realm of the dead, mimicking their state and by this action attracting them to her. Familiar spirits could come from deep within the Earth; the Witch of Endor summons up the spirit of Samuel from the Earth itself. The spirits of the dead are buried in graveyards, and we are all born from and return to the Earth; it might not be such a vast jump that somehow Earth contains all of our family for us to both draw from and return to, the great womb and tomb of all life. Earth is mother and reaper of all life upon her.

Here with the references to the womb, we can see some of the possible connections to the force of the libido. If a woman's sexuality is somehow tied to the procuring of the familiar spirit, instead of sex and childbirth, all of these ancient references to her womb and her chastity could be talking about using female sexual power to attract and house a great creator and earth spirit, instead of a great man. In the case of the Oracle of Delphi, it became known later that the special throne she sat upon revealed her naked genitals, which hovered over a crack in the earth that was leaking psychoactive gas. Here in the cave, the witch was letting a vapor from Earth into her body in a very literal fashion. It was not a spiritual possession so much as a chemical union with a "spirit" arising from deep inside Earth; the oracle absorbing this gas through her vulva and womb.

The ancient oracle tradition came to its death, in a state-sanctioned fashion at least, in 393 CE, when Theodosius made an official order that the priestesses be murdered and never permitted to resume their duties. Their temple was taken over by the priests, and women never practiced there again. Ironically, in the last prophecy given by an oracle, it was announced that Rome would fall and the empire would end. This prediction was followed by the death of Theodosius only five years later and the end of the Western Roman Empire in another fifteen years' time.

Similar types of oracles using methods congruent to the sibyls can be found in other parts of the world as well. In Tibet, for example, there was a long tradition of oracles known as the Nechung Oracle. This state oracle is a key part of Tibetan religious society and works as a close adviser to the Dalai Lama. Having some type of spiritual oracle was common practice for many political leaders and can still be found in places today. Ronald Reagan had his astrologer, just as Nicholas, the last czar of Russia, consulted Rasputin. The Nechung Oracle of Tibet is temporarily taken over, or possessed, by a familiar spirit and thus performs the same type of belly-talking technique as the sibyls. These Nechung Oracles were also considered to be protected by guardian spirits, kind of like a guardian angel, and had the responsibilities not only of providing prophecies but also means of protection.

Buddhist dance practitioner and scholar Ellen Pearlman writes:

When Padmasambhava consecrated Samye Monastery with the
Vajrakilaya dance, he tamed the local spirit protector, Pehar Gyalp,
and bound him by oath to become the head of the entire hierarchy
of Buddhist protective spirits. Pehar, later known as Dorje Drakden,
became the principal protector of the Dalai Lamas, manifesting
through the Nechung Oracle.

According to the Dalai Lama, "Tibetans rely on oracles for various reasons. The purpose of the oracles is not just to foretell the
future. They are called upon as protectors and sometimes used as
healers. However, their primary function is to protect the Buddha
Dharma and its practitioners."[6]

5

Familiar Spirits in Judeo-Christianity

Don't be drunken with wine, in which is dissipation, but be filled with the Spirit.

EPHESIANS 5:18

The Judeo-Christian religions have historically harshly judged and condemned witches who have familiar spirits, practice idolatry, and prophesy. These condemnations have led to millions of deaths and spilled the blood of far too many pagans to count. Though these religions have sometimes espoused and practiced tolerance, witches who kept familiars were not given grace and forgiven and were mostly put to death. It is stated in several passages of the Bible that these practices are taboo, and one should avoid having contact with any witch who has a familiar spirit. Nothing less than totally shunning them was acceptable. It is absolutely forbidden to consult with familiar spirits upon pain of death. Christians have come to believe, due to some passages in the Bible, that a witch actually loses her soul and is damned if she practices divination or consults the spirits of the dead. As Leviticus 20:27 states: "A man or a woman who has a ghost or a familiar spirit shall be put to death; they shall be pelted with stones—their bloodguilt shall be upon them."

On the other hand, it is common practice in all of the existing Christian churches to come into contact and communicate with the Holy Spirit and to consult with Jesus, who is dead. So a Christian can have conversations with only one spirit and one ancestor—Jesus; any other experience is expressly forbidden. In addition, there are *some* types of divination that are approved by churches and synagogues and in the Bible, and most of those can only be performed by priests. None of the divination methods performed by the priestesses were approved; they were all deemed taboo, and the practitioners were punished.

All religions have hypocritical practices, but the extent to which the Jewish and Christian religions vehemently abhor keeping familiar spirits is in stark contrast to the practices they encourage with the Holy Spirit, who they deem worthy. How do the Christian fathers know the witches are not conferring with the very same Holy Spirit as their own priests? But then that could be my familiar spirit making that judgment and tainting my consciousness with its "impure filth."

Although the Catholic Church staunchly reprimands necromancy practiced by witches, all Roman Catholic altars contain the remains of a saint, called relics, which are in fact defiling the sanctity of the church, according to the church's own admonitions. The familiar spirit of the dead messiah, Jesus Christ, is called upon during every Sunday mass. The entire cathedral of St. Peter in Rome is built upon, and calls upon, the dead buried underneath it, as it is constructed on top of a grave mound. If the pope sees fit to demonize a witch for praying in a graveyard, I suppose St. Peter's should, by the same reckoning, be evacuated immediately. A better solution might be to acknowledge this all as hypocritical rubbish so that we can all embrace the dead, our ancestors, and the past without making these practices taboo.

In 2017, Pope Francis spoke out against occult practices and diviners, mediums, and sorcerers: "'Horoscopes and necromancy' are not necessary to know the future, 'reading palms and the crystal ball' are useless: the 'true Christian' trusts God and lets himself be guided on a path open to the surprises of God. Otherwise, you cannot be a 'true

Christian' explained Pope Francis."[1] Yet the Vatican has a long history with divination practices such as augury, in which birds are watched for signs and omens. Papal inauguration ceremonies often include the release of doves. In fact, the word *inaugurate* comes from the Latin *inaugurare,* which combined *in-* with *augēre,* meaning "to increase." *Augēre* is likely the origin of *augur,* the word for an official diviner of ancient Rome, and *augury.* In ancient Rome the augur's job was to interpret signs to determine whether the gods approved of an action before it was undertaken, which is how *inaugurate* came to mean "to consecrate or induct into office with suitable ceremonies."[2] Although the church now claims that the release of doves is to symbolize the Catholic Church spreading peace in the world, it is impossible not to notice the many connections carried over from ancient Rome.

> The pope also inherited an ancient Roman priestly title, Pontifex Maximus, this too, almost certainly passed down from the Etruscans, along with Etruscan priestly paraphernalia like the folding chair we see a servant carrying in the Tomb of the Augurs. A crooked staff called the lituus (one of these also appears in the Tomb of the Augurs) eventually turned into a symbolic shepherd's crook for Christian pastors, but only long after it had been used by Etruscan priests called augurs to divine the future by scrutinizing the heavens and the flight patterns of birds.[3]

Unfortunately the pope's last few auguries did not go well. The peace doves were attacked by crows and seagulls in a very anti-peace sentiment. For myself, as a practicing witch, I can't quite come to peace with the church's persecution of pagans for the same practices sanctioned to the priests for centuries.

In Judaism, only one form of forgiveness is given to the idolaters and diviners who speak with familiar spirits, and it is given to a special group. A fascinating story of an acceptance of the use of familiar spirits is told in archaic versions of the tale of Abraham. An obscure passage tells of a "gift" that Abraham gave to the sons of his concubines. These bastard sons and their descendants, referred to as the children of the east, were given the ability to speak with demons and have relations with familiar spirits. These spirits were to be used to counsel humanity; as a result, the witches who used these powers were forgiven by God because, though they were utilizing unclean spirits, they did so to assist others, as described in Genesis 25:6: "Now Abraham gave all that he had to Isaac; but to the sons of his concubines, Abraham gave gifts while he was still living, and sent them away from his son Isaac eastward, to the land of the east."

The actual Hebrew word used for the gifts was *tumah,* and it was said that he gave them that name to use for themselves. Tumah is commonly translated as the name of the unclean spirits or impure demons—that is, familiar spirits. According to *The Encyclopedia of Jewish Myth, Magic and Mysticism:*

> Names of Impurity: (Shemot Tumah). A mysterious power that the Talmud reports Abraham bequeathed to the gentile children of his concubines. The concept may have its roots in Zechariah 13:2, where the "impurity of the land" derives from the names of idols. These children of Abraham became the fabled Children of the East, the masters of magic and astrology. This story is offered as an explanation for why non-Jews are able to perform efficacious magic. RaSHI identifies shemot tumah as knowledge of witchcraft and demonology. Later sages relate this term to some of the techniques used in exorcism.[4]

In a Hebraic context, this can mean a spirit of the dead: one of the ways someone can become "unclean" is through working with or touching the dead. So technically, this can refer to, for example, washing and dressing a corpse, burying a corpse, and worship of dead ancestors. These practices are generally not considered evil, but there are taboos and restrictions because of concerns over disease and health-related issues. In many cases in older Jewish literature, the connotation of uncleanliness or impurity in no way indicated that people could not engage with the dead; proper protocols for handling the dead were simply being indicated. The judgment of evil was imposed upon these practices at a later time through mistranslation and misunderstanding. Through a deeper understanding of the wording used by the Hebrews, we can see how the belief of many Jewish and Christian folks that conferring with the spirits of the dead is "evil" could have just been a misunderstanding of this concept of "unclean." All women who are menstruating are also considered unclean—another example of how this thinking must not be taken to extremes to judge perfectly natural occurrences, whether menstruation or death, as evil and taboo. That is all human error and ignorance, not religious dogma.

Also, if one had the misfortune of becoming unclean, it was fairly simple to remedy; all one needed to do was take a ritual bath. Far from the extreme judgment and defilement attributed to these practices, a simple baptism provided a cure-all for the state of evil imposed through all these familiar spirits in the ancient Jewish and Christian texts. So it begs the question, why all the fuss over something easily removed by a simple bath?

The children of the east reference is specific in Judaism and refers also to the sorcerers and magi. Wise men were called by this name, and they too conferred with familiar spirits all the time. In the story of the birth of Christ the three magi, or wise men, are said to have come "from the east." Without more of a context, many do not know what this is referring to. According to the old Jewish texts, as elucidated in the Zohar, the east is a place of magic and witchcraft.

[402]*land of the East*—domain of . . . impure witchcraft. The East is famous as a realm of astrology and magic.

[403]*in the mountains of the East dwell those who teach witchcraft* . . . Chief among them Uzza and Azael—two angels who opposed the creation of Adam and Eve, fell from heaven, and were attracted

by *the daughters of men*. They were punished by being bound in chains of iron in the mountains of darkness, from where they still manage to wreak havoc, teaching sorcery to humans.[5]

It was thought that these angels acted as familiar spirits to those who practiced divination and gave them instructions on how to gain superpowers and magical abilities, and in later Jewish works these spirits were considered beneficial. Solomon himself, known as the wisest man to have walked Earth, utilized the aid of demons and familiar spirits to build the Temple, after all, so there must be some means of attrition for the usage of unclean spirits in all respects, as there are exceptions to the rule found throughout Jewish history. We can see enveloped within many of our popular mythologies the presence of these others. Adam had a ministering angel, called Raziel, who gave him the book of life known as the *Sefer Raziel* (Book of Raziel), which contained all the information he would need to know.

The angel Raziel
Original art by Maja D'Aoust

When Moses ascended to heaven, it was the angels who guided him and later instructed him on how to remake the tablets he broke upon his knee. When viewed through a different lens, we see that most of the religious figures were in fact guided by some kind of spirit, be it called angel, God, the Holy Spirit, or whatever popular nomenclature one wishes to use. So why would these be distinguished so judgmentally from the familiar spirits of the witches?

6

Isis, Pandora, and the Angels of the East

The figure of Isis is sometimes used to represent the occult and magical arts, such as necromancy, invocation, sorcery, and thaumaturgy. In one of the myths concerning her, Isis is said to have conjured the invincible god of eternities, Ra, to tell her his secret and sacred name, which he did. This name is equivalent to the Lost Word of Freemasonry. By means of this word, a magician can demand obedience from the invisible and superior deities. The priests of Isis became adepts in the use of the unseen forces of nature. They understood hypnotism, mesmerism, and similar practices long before the modern world dreamed of their existence.

MANLY P. HALL, *THE SECRET TEACHINGS OF ALL AGES*

Despite all the many warnings against conferring with familiar spirits and how doing so has been denigrated in some religions, the benefits can hardly be denied, at least from the perspective of many ancient origin stories and myths. Regardless of whether you believe in familiar spirits, according to historical accounts, the information and powers they are reported to have conferred advanced human

The goddess Isis
Illustration by Athanasius Kircher, from Kircher's
Oedipus Aegyptiacus (1652)

civilization by quantum leaps, if there is any truth to these stories.

Some religious texts state that familiar spirits have no worthy information to confer to humanity, but in the majority of origin tales, all areas of knowledge and expertise—language, agriculture, science, astronomy, fine art, music, and architecture—came to the human race via familiar spirits and genius daimon guardians. These spirits, whether angels, aliens, *rishis,* or fairies, inspired modern civilization. Whatever you choose to believe about the existence or source of these forces (angels or aliens), the stories and mythologies of ancient peoples all specify that this knowledge came from supernatural or spiritual sources—or at least that was their interpretation of the phenomenon at the time.

The supernatural source of something such as language, for example, often takes the form of an angel-like creature or spirit who comes from either the stars, the sea, or from underground. The Chinese language was given to the serpent man Fu Xi by a unicorn (or *kirin*); the Greek language was given to Hermes by a giant serpent named Poimanderes. In Africa, language came from the fish people from the Dog Star, Sirius; the Native Americans procured their language from the Horned River snakes. The thing that is consistent in all these tales of incredible knowledge or ideas coming to humanity is that usually some kind of guiding force with a discernible form directed the human mind to the realization of it. Many humans who have received an epiphany—an original idea or a song—have described these kinds of experiences in great detail and sometimes credit a muse. The mystery is the identity of the assistants.

One might suppose from this that human beings are meant to work in tandem with these supernatural forces so that growth and evolution in civilization can occur—because we would never have made it this far on our own or it would have taken a lot longer. These stories of humanity gaining knowledge from another source also mimic the Prometheus myth. In this myth, humans are missing something that must be procured or stolen from the gods. Prometheus, a Titan, defies the gods by stealing fire and giving it to humans. Rather than literal fire, this could be interpreted as creative fire or light, the ability to create or conceive new thoughts from out of nowhere—a priori knowledge, as the philosopher Kant names it. In one version of the myth, Zeus, angered that Prometheus gave fire to humans, punishes the Titan by chaining him to a rock. He then instructs Hephaestus, god of fire, to make Pandora, the first woman, out of clay. The gods give her various gifts (the ability to weave and speak, fine clothing, and jewelry), including, from Zeus, a box, which he tells her not to open. But her curiosity overtakes her, and she opens it, releasing pain and suffering upon humanity but also giving them hope.

Many of us are familiar with the Prometheus myth and know about

Pandora's box, but we might not know the deeper role that Pandora plays or the significance of the box. Many scholars say that Pandora's box was much like the pithos jar described earlier, both a womb and a tomb, and that this jar was literally Pandora's womb. Robert Meagher, humanities professor at Hampshire College, explains the connections between the pithos and the story of Pandora.

> A pithos is a jar that is womb-like in shape and is a symbol for the earth, the mother of all. The implications of the pithos to the story of Pandora are obvious. Pandora's gifts are released from her own womb. Her fault lies not in her curiosity, but *in her being.* She is constitutionally deceptive and lethal because she draws men into her pithos, and brings new men forth for a life of misery. The image of Woman as a pithos is extremely ancient. In many ancient Helladic burials, the pithos was used as a coffin. The deceased was placed inside in a fetal position, covered with honey, and buried in the hope of new life and regeneration.[1]

In some versions of the story, the womb of Pandora received the fire of Prometheus, and she then gave it to humanity, who previous to this were decidedly dullards, or perhaps even apes. The exchange between Prometheus and Pandora was referred to as a gift. As noted earlier, Pandora's gift, when released, spread evil all over Earth, "infecting" humans with this present from the gods. Most humans could not handle what was let out of Pandora's womb. It is confusing how such a gift could be so terrible, but if we look into the etymology of the word *gift,* we see that it also means "poison." Could it be that this gift was somehow related to the gifts to the children of the east? The symbolism of the concubine, or surrogate, is that they offer up their womb in a sacrificial manner, and perhaps the concubines of Abraham were offering up their wombs to more than just human children but to some kind of spiritual function. If we view the story as symbolic instead of literal, there is certainly congruency happening in many of these familiar tales, with women and their wombs somehow forming a relationship with something supernatural.

When we consider the earlier chapter on the celibacy practices of witches who engage the familiar spirit this becomes very intriguing. If we view the complete story of Prometheus we see that one possible interpretation is that a creative ability is placed within the womb of Pandora from a heavenly, or supernatural, source. This creative ability is easy to interpret as the ability to reproduce, but what if there is also some other strange mystery contained within the tale that is also getting at the practices in ancient times of women reserving their wombs for the gods, as in the belly-talkers?

Portal of Pandora
Original art by Maja D'Aoust

We can also see connections between the earth goddesses and Pandora and how they relate to the womb and tomb, as stated by scholars such as Stan Kirk.

> There is also the view that the very name Pandora (literally *All-gifts*) suggests that she is essentially an earth goddess because it resembles similar epithets of Gaia and other earth goddesses. Some have boldly suggested parallels between the name *Pandora* and the first biblical woman *Eve,* claiming that both names were originally epithets of an all-giving earth goddess:

> > Eve, the first woman of the biblical myth, also seems to have been a later variant, a successor of an earlier earth-mother concept that became humanized with time. The name Eva (Havva), at the side of the too obvious term of *Išah* (išah=woman. Gen. II. 23), denoted *the mother of all the living* according to biblical interpretation (Gen. III. 20); the name thus recalls the similar attributes of Ge with Hesiod (*pantôn mētēr, Erga* 563) and with Aeschylus (*pammētôr, Prom.* 88). [Trenscényi-Waldapfel 1955, 107]

> It has more specifically been argued that there is a parallel between the meaning of *Pandora* and Eve's epithet in Genesis as well as a plausible link between Eve and demoted Mesopotamian creation goddesses, and that this link indicates a Near Eastern pattern of demoting mother goddesses similar to that which is supposedly evident in the demotion of Pandora:

> > Like Eve's name, Pandora's appears to be an onomastic form of earth. It appears to have been severed as . . . the others were from an earth goddess to which it had early been attached. But, Pandora, like Eve, has been transformed into the name of the first woman of her race. . . . The all- nurturing creatress has been transmogrified into a seductive subhuman creature, the ultimate demotion. [O'Brien 1983, 39–40][2]

These stories could be a metaphor for a real biological evolution of the leap from ape to man if viewed through a different perspective. They could be indicative of some superconsciousness that humans are gaining access to at periodic intervals through different techniques or random happenstance. They could also be only stories made to explain away a mystery. No matter what the truth is behind any of these explanations, we can look closely at all the possibilities and invite a more complete perspective on the subject.

In a very special text titled "Isis the Prophetess to Her Son Horus" written by the Greek alchemist Zosimos, it is related that all of the alchemical knowledge of chemistry, language, healing, agriculture, and metallurgy came about entirely because one woman, Isis, developed relationships with familiar spirits. Isis sought out the information on purpose and knowingly solicited these spirits. She sacrificed her body to have sexual relations with an angel to procure the knowledge and wisdom of these arts. In this ancient volume, it is related that civilization in addition to alchemy was given to humans by way of the relationship between Isis and this angel, or guardian spirit, whom she drew to her through her desire to know. One could infer that nothing less than the development of Egyptian civilization came from relationships with familiar spirits, and that is pretty undeniably epic. Psychologist and astrologer Monika Wikman tells the story, in her book *Pregnant Darkness,* of how Isis met and interacted with these angels.

In the Ancient Egyptian text titled *Isis to Horus, or The Prophetess Isis to Her Son*—to which both Jung and von Franz refer in their work—Isis, imaged in one of her forms as an adept alchemist, meets with the angel who knows the alchemical art. Before this meeting occurs, however, a different angel comes. This angel wants to have intercourse with her, but Isis wants to know the secrets of the art, so she puts off his sexual advances. When she demands the knowledge from him, he tells her that he is not permitted to speak about the mysteries because of their supreme importance. He leaves, telling her that the next day an angel would arrive with the solution to the problem. Isis says he also spoke of the sign of this angel—"He bore it on his head and would show me a small, unpitched vessel filled with a translucent water. He would tell me the truth."

The next day an angel greater than the first, Amnael, appears before her with the vessel, and he, too, is full of desire for Isis. Again, Isis begins inquiring into the matter. The angel reveals the secret—the vessel and the waters and recipes—which she can pass on to her son, Horus.[3]

The two angels mentioned in the above passage seem similar to the angels of the east mentioned earlier in the Abraham tale of the children of the east, where he sends his concubines to learn magic from two specific angels who dwell on a certain mountain. Perhaps Isis was one such concubine who entreated the angels for the same knowledge of how to confer with familiar spirits. Here, in this excerpt from "Isis the Prophetess to Her Son Horus," Isis speaks directly to Horus.

For that the sources of all things wrought on the earth by word or deed, are up above, and they dispense for us their essences by weight and measure; and there is naught which hath not come down from above, and will return again to re-descend.

14. What dost thou mean again by this, my mother? Tell me!

And Isis once again did make reply: Most holy Nature hath set in living creatures the clear sign of this return. For that this breath which we breathe from above out of the air, we send out up again, to take it in [once more].[4]

7

The Witch Watchers

Those who restrain desire do so because theirs is weak enough to be restrained.

WILLIAM BLAKE,
THE MARRIAGE OF HEAVEN AND HELL

The sexual desire and attraction between the guardian spirits and human females is an issue in the annals of human history. Tales of these liaisons fill ancient literature. In the Jewish Bible it was said that the angels appointed to "watch over" the humans were called the watchers, or Grigori. These watchers had sexual relationships with the women they were supposed to be taking care of, which compromised their authority. These physical relationships not only transferred knowledge but also produced children who were known as the Nephilim, who promptly wrecked and corrupted humankind, inspiring the great flood to cleanse Earth of them, as the story goes. The Book of Enoch explores this phenomenon and familiar occurrence.

Since much is written on the Book of Enoch, I will only touch briefly on it here, looking into some more esoteric references drawn from it. The Book of Enoch was made taboo by Jewish rabbis, and people were encouraged not to read it. Enoch had a familiar spirit, an angel, who related the information to him and guided him through heaven, where the angels showed and educated him on the ways of heaven. Lynn

Osburn, a longtime student of alchemy, describes how Enoch was taken to heaven.

> The Book of Enoch describes how he was taken to the heavens after a tour of the earth: "The Lord spoke, 'Have no fear, Enoch, good man and scribe of goodness. Come hear my voice. Go speak to the Watchers of Heaven, who have sent you to intercede for them. Tell them: You should intercede for men, and not men for you. Why did you leave lofty, holy Heaven to sleep with women, to defile yourselves with the daughters of men and take them as your wives? . . .'" After God's rhetorical admonition against his lustful yet loving angels He said to Enoch, "As for the Watchers who sent you to intercede for them, tell them: 'You were in Heaven but the mysteries were not revealed to you. You knew worthless ones, and in the hardness of your hearts you revealed these to women, and through these secrets women and men work much evil [on] earth.' Say to them, 'You have no peace.'"[1]

The specifics and intrigues of these dramas are all well recorded, especially in Jewish apocryphal literature, but I would like to focus on relationships that have developed between women and angels. Some of these relationships resulted not in destructive forces but in positive outcomes, such as those of Isis, who helped the entire civilization of Egypt. There were apparently different kinds of watchers: some were fallen and some weren't. In other words, not all the watchers became corrupted, though even the *unfallen* watchers engaged in sexual relationships, which contradicted my initial thought that they were defiled because they had sex. I discovered a deeper significance to these unions, especially the relationships of the unfallen angels.

In kabbalistic sources, I found two other names for these watchers, other than the Grigori: Kaddishin (also Kiddishin) and Irin Qaddism, which both mean "Holy Ones." According to the *Jewish Encyclopedia,* these watchers sit in judgment from the loftiest position of all—next to God on his throne.

[Enoch] describes the "Irin and Kaddishin," who daily sit in judgment with God. . . . [Enoch] leads [Moses] up through the seven heavens. . . . [In the] sixth heaven, [Moses sees] the "Irin and Kaddishin"; in the seventh, 'Arabot, he sees first the angels "Wrath and Anger," then the angel of death, then the hayyot standing before God, and finally an angel engaged in teaching the souls.[2]

There is surprisingly little data on these benevolent angelic beings, whereas much more attention is focused on their more negative counterparts, the fallen ones who produced the Nephilim. In apocryphal literature, they hold a high office in the angelic hierarchy. They communicated directly with humans and, as familiar spirits, provided protection and guidance to messiahs. Gnostic scholar Tau Malachi describes these exalted angels.

These are primordial and supernal angels that are among those exalted beyond Archangel Metatron, and so they are most lofty and holy among the angels of El Elyon. You may recall the images of the kerubim on the ark of covenant that appeared as "twin angels," both the Irin and the Kaddishin are twin angels, and so they constitute four emanations of Supernal Judgment. These primordial and supernal angels, however, do not resemble anything like kerubim, but their emanations are such that they cannot be described, and there are very few among the tzaddikim in the Messiah that can gaze upon them.[3]

Perhaps these unfallen watchers are like the spirit mates described in alchemical texts—texts that were inspired by the myth of Isis joining with angels. A true soul mate is a spirit on high with whom one develops a relationship of trust and commitment that culminates in a sacred marriage. The stories of these apparent sexual relationships and marriages could be a way of symbolically representing or describing a spiritual transformation.

These ideas are interpreted in highly sexual terms in Kabbalah, regarding which we are informed that *"sexual intimacy* within the life of God is the paradigmatic expression of divine wholeness." In this regard I stated that just as the human sexual act itself is "employed with the intention of encouraging a 'Sacred Marriage'" between the masculine and feminine aspects of the Divine One, the visualization and mental expression of . . . (*Yahadonnahi*) is equally understood to facilitate the said 'Sacred Marriage.'"

There are however two important Divine Name constructs comprised of the conjunctions. . . . The second Divine Name construct pertains to *"Kadishim"* (Sanctifications), and refers to "the return of the Light." Hence like the "Lunar Principle," it is the "Reflected Light" from *Malchut* to *Tiferet,* which takes place when we say *Kadish* for the dead.[4]

In the traditional interpretations of the Book of Enoch, and of the watchers, they are presented as evil beings spreading evil over Earth, much like the spirits springing from Pandora's box. They fell from heaven because of their lust for sex and are corrupt. These interpretations are in stark contrast to the sacred marriages with women described elsewhere in Jewish literature. In these other versions, the watchers still seemed to have intercourse with women, but they never fell from grace and in fact were right next to God's throne. The only difference I could find is that they were married; the sex happened within the context of holy matrimony. I did find an odd passage that talked about how the Grigori did not have wives and were not permitted to have wives in heaven. But somehow this other group were allowed to have human wives, and their stories were very different.

I discovered yet another name for them: the Iyr. This very interesting Hebraic word means a kind of sentinel or citadel, a watcher, someone who stands guard over something like a sentry or soldier. *Strong's Greek and Hebrew Dictionary of the Bible* defines *iyr* as "a city (a place guarded by waking or a watch) in the widest sense (even of a mere encampment or post)."[5] Genesis 4:17 says of Cain, "he built a city, and called the name of the city, after the name of his son, Enoch." In the Genesis passage the word for city is *iyr,* so it means that Cain built a city of watchers, or sentinels, for Enoch. Some interpret it to mean that Cain provided Enoch with guardian angels. This then begins Enoch's relationship with the watchers and sentinel angels discussed at length in the Book of Enoch.

The notion of a watchful guardian spirit or angel reminded me of the Great Sphinx in Giza. The sphinx is a very real watcher and guardian, literally and eternally watching the sun rise in the east. This felt like an echo of the same concept to me. The ancient Egyptians called the Great Sphinx by various names, among them Seshep-ankh Atum, which means "the living image of the god Atum,"[6] and Hayyot, which means "holy living creature."[7] Hayyot is also the name of a class of heavenly creatures known as the cherubim, which are minor guardian deities. In modern Egyptian Arabic, the sphinx is called Abü al Hül, the "terrifying one" or "father of terror." Truly, the sphinx is the guardian of the children of the east, as it faces that direction for eternity. The sphinx is perhaps one of the most impressive guardian spirits ever idolized of all time. A perfect presentation of the epitome of the familiar.

The Great Sphinx—a lion with the head of a man—guarding the pyramid tombs of Giza also seems related to the two lions always shown with the earth goddess Cybele, progenitor of the sibyls. As noted earlier, the sphinx is related to Atum, an Egyptian creator god who is much like Cybele, the creator of life, the womb and tomb. In Egyptian mythology, Atum fashions humanity from the clay of Earth. Some scholars theorize that at one time a second sphinx guarded the gateway of the pyramids, the two making a pair. And pairs of lions are usually found at the doors of every temple in Egypt, just as there are double lions guarding the doors of most temples and buildings all over China. Perhaps these lion spirits guard the Eastern spirits of the angels who contain the knowledge of sorcery. The sphinx seems to be guarding the city of these angels, where they reside. Perhaps Isis and Osiris are a witch and wizard who achieved the greatest magical level, acquiring the highest guardians known to humans, the *kerubim* and the Kaddishin, primordial guardian familiars of the *hieros gamos*. Some affiliate the symbol of these double lions to life itself and regeneration, as Dr. Zahi Hawass, an Egyptian archaeologist, Egyptologist, and former Minister of State for Antiquities Affairs explains:

> The idea is expressed in the association between Atum and Ruti, the double lion god who is somewhat like a cell that has doubled its elements and begun to divide, before the actual split has occurred. The double lion also alludes to Shu and Tefnut, the first differentiation of Atum's being. But Ruti says, "I am the double lion, older than Atum," so appearing even before the actual birth of the next primordial generation.[8]

Offspring
Original art by Maja D'Aoust

The fact that there are so many versions and forms of sexual inter-actions and marriages between humans and strange spirits might seem flabbergasting, but if one were to pay attention to the fact that one of the world's largest religions, Christianity, is actually based entirely on the concept that a spirit comes to a human and impregnates her, we see that this is a very commonly held belief even today. Some Christians, for example, are shocked by the stories of the ancient pagans and con-sider these "heathen" beliefs evil, without recognizing that the story they believe in is pretty much the same thing. In my opinion there is little difference between the stories of these early women who had intercourse with spirits and bore offspring and that of Mary, who is impregnated by the Holy Spirit and gives birth to Jesus Christ. Since her offspring is seen as a positive contribution to humanity, unlike the Nephilim, perhaps this was an example of the hieros gamos.

8

The Holy Spirit
versus Succubi and Incubi

The angel replied, "The Holy Spirit will come upon you,
and the power of the Most High will overshadow you. So,
the Holy One to be born will be called the Son of God."

LUKE 1:35

The story of Mary's interactions with the Holy Spirit also involved angelic entities; the angel Gabriel came to her before the Holy Spirit paid her a visit to inform her of what was going to happen. Given that Mary is a virgin, this suggests some kind of relationship between the libido and the attraction of the familiar spirit because, according to the story, Mary was a virgin, like the vestal virgins of Rome, who existed long before Mary met up with the Holy Spirit. For those unaware of the whole history of belly-talkers and women being impregnated by angels, this story of Mary and the Holy Spirit might seem like a one-off, until you become aware of the long history of manuscripts dating into antiquity containing this same tale. The fact that the Prometheus myth mentions the womb of Pandora, which takes in the creative spirit of the familiars, daimons, or angels—whatever you choose to name them— has implications, in my opinion, when considering the impregnation of Mary by the Holy Spirit. The parallels between the creative fire of the gods entering the womb of Pandora and Mary having God's child seem apparent enough to me. Whether this connection to the familiar is for communicating information or for having children and establishing *family* relations with a spirit remains to be determined.

How, then, can we not see that Mary the virgin is only a mirror of these ancient tales of those women who chose to be chaste to attract a spirit so that they could come under its protection and guardianship and bear its fruits. Mary, however, apparently did not choose to do these practices but instead was chosen, according to the literature.

Mary was not the only woman made pregnant by God's agency in the Bible, although she seems to be the winner of the popularity contest from a religious and cultural perspective. In the story of Abraham and Sarah, Sarah is sterile and cannot have a child, thus the need for the concubines who bore the children of the east. But God visits her and assures her that he will help her have a child, which eventually came to pass when, late in life, she gave birth to Isaac. There is some controversy as to whether God or Abraham was the father of Isaac. A Jewish philosopher, Philo of Alexandria, wrote a lot on the subject; he believed that God visited Sarah and impregnated her much in the same way that the Holy Spirit visited Mary, impregnating her with Jesus. Apparently, in biblical lore, this was not an isolated incident. References to children being born in this fashion would certainly threaten the Christian concept that Jesus was the Lord's only begotten son, and yet there are seemingly several of these conceptions and births mentioned in Jewish literature, such as in the works of Philo.

When happiness, that is Isaac, was born, she says, in the pious exaltation, "The Lord has caused me laughter, and whoever shall hear of it shall rejoice with Me." Open your ears, therefore, O ye initiated, and receive the most sacred mysteries. Laughter is joy; and the expression "has caused" is equivalent to "has begotten." So that what is here said has some such meaning as this, "The Lord has begotten Isaac."[1]

There were, surprisingly, a number of biblical figures who were the offspring of either God or an angel. Noah's father, Lamech, was convinced that God was the father of Noah and not himself. Elizabeth, Mary's cousin, was, like Sarah, infertile and told by God that she would have a child. According to an account in the Book of Luke, Mary was in the middle of getting ready to marry Joseph when she learned from Gabriel that she would bear God's child. She was terrified that this would ruin her marriage and ran to Elizabeth to tell her. Elizabeth said the same thing had happened to her and that Mary shouldn't worry. Elizabeth had been trying to have a child for a long time when Gabriel visited her and told her that she would become pregnant—which she promptly did. Mary stayed with her cousin for a while, and when she returned to Joseph, she was pregnant. A tricky situation for Joseph, I'm sure. The following passages from Luke (1:26–28, 1:35–38) describe the situation.

Six months after Elizabeth knew she was to become a mother, Gabriel was sent from God to Nazareth. Nazareth was a town in the country of Galilee. 27 He went to a woman who had never had a man. Her name was Mary. She was promised in marriage to a man named Joseph. Joseph was of the family of David. 28 The angel came to her and said, "You are honored very much. You are a favored woman. The Lord is with you. You are chosen from among many women." . . . 34 Mary said to the angel, "How will this happen? I have never had a man." 35 The angel said to her, "The Holy Spirit will come on you. The power of the Most High will cover you. The holy Child you give birth to will be called the Son of God. 36 See, your cousin Elizabeth, as old as she is, is going to give birth to a child. She was not able to have children before, but now she is in her sixth month. 37 For God can do all things." 38 Then Mary said, "I am willing to be used of the Lord. Let it happen to me as you have said." Then the angel went away from her.

The Holy Spirit is obviously the preferred familiar spirit as its off-spring seems to be more desirable than the Nephilim, who destroyed everything and ate people. Jesus, in opposition to the cannibalistic practices of the Nephilim, instead fed his own body to people, quite a contrast. In the same tradition of Isis, Mary engaged with an angel who gave her information and then gave birth to offspring who changed humanity. If we take out the Christian judgment that Mary is "good" whereas Isis is merely pagan, it is not too difficult to draw parallels between the tales.

SUCCUBI AND INCUBI AS FAMILIAR SPIRITS

An incubus or succubus can be harmless, or it can be destructive. Like any sexual situation, the danger depends on how you handle it. . . . All sex is potentially dangerous. . . . Our sexual feelings make us vulnerable. How many people have been ruined by a sexual partner? Sex does provide a point of invasion and the incubi and succubi simply make us intensely aware of this.

WILLIAM BURROUGHS IN VICTOR BOCKRIS,
WITH WILLIAM BURROUGHS: A REPORT FROM THE BUNKER

Along with the stories of beneficial familiars are tales of sexual intercourse with terrifying spirits—the succubi and incubi. Just as we sometimes have human mates who are abusive or unpleasant, the same can be true of familiar spirits, according to the stories of the succubi and incubi. It seems that some people attract familiar spirits who have a harsh nature and are not exactly ideal mates, but these spirits serve them regardless of their violent qualities. For hundreds of years, both males and females have spoken of spiritual visitors who assaulted them sexually, a type of spirit rape. In the case of the female succubus or male incubus, the human is approached in a controlling fashion and forced to engage the spirit. These are also somewhat affectionately called demon lovers.

A demon making love to a witch
Anonymous woodcut, from Ulrich Molitor, *De laniis*
et phitonicis mulierbus (1493)

Although the tale of Mary being visited by the Holy Spirit seems very spiritual, in descriptions of her encounter, Mary didn't seem to have had much choice in the matter. An angel did come down and at least have the courtesy to inform her that the event would occur, but I didn't read the part where she gave consent; she seems terrified, which is very similar to stories about the succubi and incubi. Succubi and incubi are called evil, even by modern Christians who have lots of ways to combat and judge them, while they worship a spirit who forced itself upon a woman. The stories of these weird spirits visiting women also mirror most of the human lovers of the god Zeus in the Greek myths. Zeus doesn't really ask his lovers, and he often assumed different forms, shapeshifting into animals and even a golden shower to accomplish the union. Some of the lovers of Zeus were more than willing to accept such a godly visit, but not all. Though the familiars still serve the humans—they seduce and grant them supernatural powers—these supernatural relationships can have a negative impact on the human participants. They can be draining to their life force and dangerous for their mental health, regardless of the powers gained.

One of the prototypes of the stories of demon lovers comes from the tale of Adam's first wife, Lilith. Similar to the stories of Mary and Joseph, Abraham and Sarah, and Isis and Osiris, wherein the wives were impregnated by angels or gods, Lilith was seduced by an angel spirit. According to one version of this ancient story, Adam Kadmon, a primordial human, was split in two, creating two separate entities. One half became Adam, and the other became Lilith. Lilith came into existence as her own entity and was not subservient to Adam. She was not really interested in hanging out with him and ran away. God ordered the angels Senoi, Sansenoi, and Sammangelof to go after Lilith and subdue her. (These angels' names are still used in Hebrew folk culture to protect children from death at the hands of Lilith and can be found engraved in placards placed above children's beds.) The angels were unsuccessful in capturing Lilith, and she became a wanton succubus who drained men and ate children. It was after this incident that God made Eve from the rib of Adam to replace Lilith, who had abandoned him to be with her familiar spirits. Lilith became the one we don't talk about, the unintegrated dark mother or dark feminine.

According to Jewish apocryphal literature, Lilith left Adam to engage with three angels—Naamah, Azza, and Azazael, and then haunted Adam at night, giving him wet dreams as she became the first succubus. Poor Adam had to deal with two difficult women. Later Eve was seduced by the serpent, who some believe represents the angel Lucifer, and when she became pregnant with Cain, she made an announcement that God was the father: "Eve names Cain and explains his name by saying, 'I have created a man with YHWH' (קניתי איש את-יהוה)" (Gen. 4:1).

Adam had to compete with these familiar spirits who visited his women and influenced them in their decisions against him. Looked at

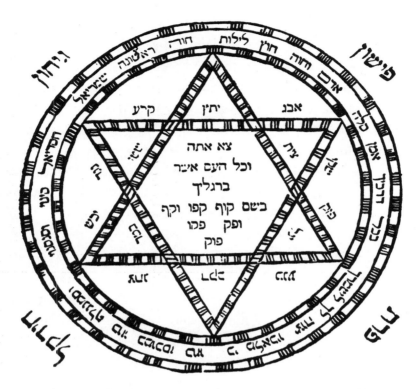

Protection spell with the names of the angels who ward off Lilith:
Senoi, Sansenoi, and Sammangelof
From the *Sefer Raziel,* an ancient Jewish text dating back
to the thirteenth century

one way, it would seem that the women of Adam cheated on him with supernatural entities.

Lilith was the original baby-eating succubus. The Hebrew name Lilith is translated as either "night" or "spirit of the air." Lilith was a popular figure, existing mainly in Semitic cultures. She had the ability to shapeshift, much like the shamanic nagual and Zeus, and was shown in some pictures standing upon two lions, exactly like Cybele.

Many people know Lilith today as the scorned first wife of Adam, who is mentioned only once in the Bible. The idea of Lilith as the first wife of Adam comes from a medieval reference in an anonymous text known as "The Alphabet of Ben Sira," written between the eighth and eleventh centuries. This text is also the origin of the story of the succubus who comes to men at night and gives them wet dreams, as it elaborates: "And she roams the world and finds children liable for punishment and she caresses them and kills them . . . and she goes and roams the world at night and makes sport with men and causes them to emit seed."[2]

From Lilith's aetheric visits to Adam in the night are spawned many demons who were said to become the incubi and succubi that would afflict humans ever after that. Even in modern times there are wards against her and fear that she may still enter into men.

In these stories, the offspring involved—namely the Nephilim, generated from a human woman who consorted with angels—were very negative and destructive; they ate people and caused a lot of problems. According to many legends, the Nephilim were thought to make demons who then haunted humans and forced themselves on them sexually in the form of incubi and succubi. Even though this seems less than delightful, and the incubi and succubi were most often uninvited guests, there are individuals who seek out these types of demon lovers on purpose to accomplish various nefarious tasks. Books on black magic have many methods for procuring this type of relationship with spirits identified as succubi and incubi. On the negative side, these types of spirits are usually obsessive-compulsive in nature and can imbue the human lover with these same qualities. Many forms of addiction and obsessive thoughts can result from these negative energy forms, which tend to spiral down and can occasionally lead to suicide.

9

Fairy Familiars

There was a man who lived not long ago near Port Erin who had a Lhiannan-Shee. "He was like other people, but he had a fairy sweetheart; but he noticed her, and they do not like being noticed, the fairies, and so he lost his mind. Well, he was quite quiet like other people, but at night he slept in the barn, and they used to hear him talking to his sweetheart, and scolding her sometimes; but if anyone made a noise he would be quiet at once." Now, the truth of this story is clear enough. The man went mad, but this madness took the form of the popular belief, and that again attributed his madness to the airy mistress. I am convinced that this was believed to be a case of genuine fairy intercourse, and it shows that the fairy creed still survives in the Isle of Man.

J. F. CAMPBELL IN A. W. MOORE,
THE FOLK-LORE OF THE ISLE OF MAN

Socrates, who was deeply intimate with his familiar spirit, used to take his pupils out into nature to sit quietly in the woods. If you try this yourself, you will quickly realize that a kind of overall sentience exists there. The overwhelming feeling of life and living things can be deeply felt when you open your heart to it. Ancient cultures believed that everything, both animate and inanimate, has a consciousness and awareness, including planet Earth as a whole, and this worldview provides the basis for the fairy faith. More than just a religious dogma, it is an experiential natural panentheistic philosophy.

The Celtic fairy world is large and old, existing almost like another dimension, and is inhabited by a wide variety of familiars. In many of the pagan traditions, the angelic intelligences had earthly forms as well as celestial, and these were called fairies. Most of the oldest tales of fairies can be traced back to Celtic and Druidic traditions. These were pagan panentheistic cultures who believed in nature worship. The scholar W. Y. Evans-Wentz described the Celtic fairy faith as not Celtic at all but more of a prehistoric animistic spirituality. The Celtic fairy faith tells the same story as most of the world's religions—of supernatural or spiritual beings coming to Earth and mating with people.

Fairies are difficult to define precisely as they take on so many forms; the fairies really contain several taxonomic systems. Professor of anthropology Dennis Gaffin, Ph.D., describes some of these different forms.

There have been some academic discussions of anthropologists' own recognitions of and experiences of various kinds of spirits, nature-spirits, discarnate beings, other-than-human-beings and other intermediate entities or energies between humans and God, the Creator, or the Prime Mover. As Wilikie (1994:164) states in Young's and Goulet's edited book on the anthropology of extraordinary experience, in a discussion of the "spirited imagination," the autonomy of spirits, and the make-up of the "inner worlds," "Some spirits are indeed figments of the human imagination, yet there are others who have been around much longer than human beings. Among spirits there is a vast hierarchy, from simple energy-forms and nature spirits to angelic and higher forms of divine and galactic intelligence. These may be terrestrial or celestial, intimately associated with human life or not, but all are aspects of the one Universal Being, conceived of as the totality, inner and outer, or as its creator."[1]

In the oldest tales, the fairies were said to be born from the fallen angels. According to the legend, as the angels fell from heaven, they landed in various places, and God froze them in place. Some landed in fire, some in the earth, some in water, and some in air. The angels became entangled in the material physical world, and thus the fairies were born.

As noted earlier, the word *fairy* is related to the goddess of fate, who gives one his lot in life, or destiny. In ancient Greek mythology, three Fates wove the web of life, described as a spider's web or a matrix that contained the past, present, and future of the world. Our "lot in life" was determined by our fate and could be revealed by our familiar spirits and the fairies of Celtic myths who were the harbingers of our fates. Most of the divinations people sought in olden times regarded relationships—particularly whether a relationship was in accordance with one's fate or destiny. One's fortune, guided by the Roman goddess Fortuna, was also directly related to betrothal and marriage. A dowry was a fortune that could be earned through a fated relationship. Interesting the marriage reference here, which seems an echo of the holy marriage and hieros gamos component of the soul mate. The word *fairy* could also mean "spirit bride," when viewed through this word meaning. There were even pagan references to making libido fetishes from the idols of fairies or the fate goddesses in the same way the pagans used idol worship to form a relationship with the spirit. Barbara G. Walker, in her encyclopedia of myths, recounts the following tale.

A legend repeated by the gypsies said if a man found the statue of a naked *fate* (fairy) in the ruins of pagan temples or tombs, he should embrace it with love and eject semen on it. Then, like Pygmalion's Galatea, the *fate* would come to life in his dreams and tell her lover where to find buried treasure, and she would become his "fortune."

He would be happy with her forevermore, provided he agreed never to set foot in a Christian church again as long as he lived.[2]

Amazing parallels can be drawn between certain fairy elements and the stories of the sibyls in terms of the sexual familiar phenomenon. In both cases we find a mythology of some form of supernatural entity that dwells inside the Earth and forms sexual relationships with humans. In the fairy tales a fairy queen who lives inside the Earth takes human lovers; in the tales of the sibyls a masculine deity enters the women who go inside the Earth's caves. Both the fairy queen and the sibyls, with their connection to the goddess Cybele, reside within the Earth's caverns and rule the underworld, connecting us with the dead and our ancestors. There are the famous fairy mounds in Ireland and Scotland, some of which are said to house the oldest human ancestors and family graveyards in the area. The fairy stories constantly reference the fairies inhabiting the graves of the forefathers, making their dwellings in what many would consider "unclean" habitats.

In *The Woman's Encyclopedia of Myths and Secrets*, Walker writes:

The Welsh knew their ancestors had a matriarchal society. Like the Irish, they called fairies the Mothers. . . . Fairies came out of their fairy hills at Halloween, Celtic folk said, because the hills themselves were tomb-wombs of rebirth. . . . The fairy queen was obviously the ancient fertility-mother, like Demeter or Ceres. . . . She was also called Diana, Venus, Hecate, Sibyl or Titania—a title of Cretan Rhea as ruler of the earth-spirits called Titans.[3]

I must interject here that, remarkably, as I was writing this passage, I was messaged on Instagram by my friend Myla Owl, who was visiting Avalon. She sent me a picture of herself in the doorway of St. Michael's Tower on top of Glastonbury Tor, home of the fairy queen Morgan la Fey. The tor is said to be the gateway between the worlds, connecting our realm to Avalon, the lost land of the fairies. She sent the following message

Emblem L: The dragon kills the woman, and she kills it,
and together they bathe in the blood.
Copperplate engraving by Matthäus Merian, from Michael Maier,
Atalanta Fugiens (1617)

with the picture: "The angel winds and voices calling out in their thun-
derous voices. They called the Tor the gateway to the Underworld. They
said the saint of cemeteries whom the Tor belongs to fought the devil and
won. . . . In consequence the devil won't touch the dead in cemeteries. . . .
The Tor is the house of the Saint." She had no idea that I was currently
writing this material, and it was a fantastic synchronicity.

The Titans were the giants, much like the Nephilim who ran amok,
and their tales mimic closely the fairy stories of the giants. When one
looks in depth at the giants in the Book of Enoch and compares them
to the European giant fables, it becomes apparent how much breadth
these stories covered. According to the dictionary definition of *fate*, the
word can also be interpreted as an oracle with a familiar spirit, or as a

Hecate
Original art by Maja D'Aoust

witch with a familiar spirit, so we see how the fairies are closely related to the ancient priestesses indeed.

> **fate (n.)** late 14c., "one's lot or destiny; predetermined course of life"; also "one's guiding spirit," from Old French *fate* and directly from Latin *fata* . . . neuter plural of *fatum* "prophetic declaration of what must be, oracle, prediction," thus the Latin word's usual sense, "that which is ordained, destiny, fate," literally "thing spoken (by the gods)," from neuter past participle of *fari* "to speak," from PIE root *bha- (2) "to speak, tell, say."[4]

Fairies have a long tradition of mating with humans. These human-fairy alliances give weight to the notion that familiar spirits are part of the human family, as fairies are literally our relatives, according to these stories. Although scholars tend to view the concept of a familiar or angel soul mate as a metaphor or imaginary friend, many cultures tell stories of how we mixed our genes with these entities through sexual relations; the specific intention of including them as part of the human family tree becomes quite apparent. Through the cultures of Europe, China, and India, as I will illustrate, the familiars, in animal, plant, and supernatural forms, are *also* our ancestors. Tales all over Europe detail love affairs of both men and women with the fairy realm, extending for hundreds if not thousands of years.

In an echo of the Nephilim stories, often these matings led to offspring. Fairy bloodlines were recorded even in some family Bibles. A human child was claimed to be stolen and left in place was a changeling, a fairy child. The kidnapped human children became spouses of the fairies; some became fairy kings and queens. The changelings, meanwhile, married humans.

Although not very scientific in terms of evidence, there are hundreds of anecdotal accounts recorded by scholars such as W. Y. Evans-Wentz, who tirelessly documented these claims. Many of the families who had interbred or had changeling experiences acknowledged this lineage through symbols in their coats of arms. Evans-Wentz, in his work *The Fairy-Faith in Celtic Countries,* states that the coat of arms for the Isle of Man, which has three legs joined at the hip in a triangle, was one such symbol. Several coats of arms indicated that a family had fairies as its familiar spirits, much like a totem pole of the Native Americans. These coats of arms depicted which fairies were the guardians of the families and possibly their blood ancestors. The intermingling of human and fairy families is an old tale.

A second account of this nature I had from a woman to whose offspring the fairies seemed to have a particular fancy. The fourth or fifth night after she was delivered of her first child, the family were alarmed by a most terrible cry of fire, on which every body ran out of the house to see whence it proceeded, not excepting the nurse, who, being as much frighted as the others, made one of the number. The poor woman lay trembling in her bed alone, unable to help herself, and her back being turned to the infant, saw not that it was taken away by an invisible hand. Those who had left her having enquired about the neighbourhood, and finding there was no cause for the outcry they had heard, laughed at each other for the mistake; but as they were going to re-enter the house, the poor babe lay on the threshold, and by its cries preserved itself from being trod upon. This exceedingly amazed all that saw it, and the mother being still in bed, they could ascribe no reason for finding it there, but having been removed by fairies, who by their sudden return, had been prevented from carrying it any farther. . . . a poor, lean, withered, deformed creature. It lay quite naked, but the clothes belonging to the child that was exchanged for it lay wrapt up all together on the bed. This creature lived with them near the space of nine years, in all which time it eats nothing except a few herbs, nor was ever seen to void any other excrement than water. It neither spoke nor could stand or go, but seemed enervate in every joint, like the changeling I mentioned before, and in all its actions showed itself to be of the same nature.[5]

FAIRY FAMILIARS AS ANCESTORS

The great majority of men in cities are apt to pride themselves on their own exemption from "superstition," and to smile pityingly at the poor countrymen and countrywomen who believe in fairies. But when they do so they forget that, with all their own admirable progress in material invention, with all the far-reaching data of their acquired science, with all the vast extent of their commercial and economic conquests,

*they themselves have ceased to be natural. . . . They have lost
all sympathetic and responsive contact with Nature, because
unconsciously they have thus permitted conventionality and
unnaturalness to insulate them from it.*

W. Y. Evans-Wentz,
The Fairy-Faith in Celtic Countries

Some scholars have theorized that fairies were members of conquered races who were either giants or pygmies or some other kind of early hominid. Some have put forward the theory that these different races of early humanoids looked so bizarre that they were mistaken for supernatural beings by *Homo sapiens.* Imagine running into something like a yeti, or an African pygmy. Someone who had never before seen a kind of human like that might not know what to think of them. Perhaps they would mistake a pygmy for a leprechaun. So, there is a chance that these fairies are our dead ancestors, early hominids now extinct. It's nevertheless interesting to think that they, after all, are included in the family of man, and so we somehow have access to them in the astral realm, as we are all blood relatives.

At the dawn of humanity, there were a variety of hominids on Earth, many of them interbreeding, according to some theories. From *Gigantopithecus,* the extinct giant ape who lived in India and may be the source for the stories of giants, to *Homo floresiensis,* the tiny hominids living on Flores, some of these early relatives of *Homo sapiens* may fit the description of at least some of the fairies who comprise the legends. The Pan-Africanist historian John G. Jackson wrote a book called *Christianity before Christ* in which he mentions that pygmy fossils have been found throughout the world, not just in Africa, and goes on to say that pygmies were most likely the founders of the human race. This theory has been echoed in other people's writings, including Charles Darwin, who determined that the pygmies were likely responsible for the race of man. Then in 1974, paleoanthropolgist Donald Johanson discovered Lucy (*Australopithecus afarensis*), who, according to one theory, was a pygmy and one of the common matriarchs for many human species.

The pygmy is arguably the closest to the brownies and leprechauns. The brownies were from an old Scottish tradition and were described as little men who showed up at night and did good deeds for you, unless you saw them, in which case they would likely play tricks on you. They were called brownies because they were dark brown and covered with hair. In October 2004 the BBC reported that scientists had discovered another species of early hominid called *Homo floresiensis* on the island of Flores in Indonesia, which they nicknamed the Hobbit. These fossils date back to about seventeen thousand years ago, so fairly recent. These Hobbit people were very small, smaller than pygmies; full-grown adults stood only three and a half feet tall. They were dark brown and covered with hair. On Flores, legends of little people abound, and descriptions of them are almost identical to those of leprechauns. The island people call them Ebu Gogo and say that they murmur to each other in some language that the Indonesians do not understand. The Ebu Gogo can also repeat what people say to them, so they are able to parrot language.

Stories of the leprechauns abound and are filled with rich details. They were small and had long beards. The leprechaun is the national fairy of Ireland. *Leprechaun* is an Old Irish word that means "little body." Leprechauns are a little insidious in that they were always known to be intoxicated; the leprechauns had a home brew that they called *poutine,* which was a little bit like mead or honey beer. The leprechauns were guardian spirits said to guard gold—a treasure left by the Danes.

Sometimes the fairy women were presented in a very idealized fashion, being more desirable than a human mate.

> *Till, clear and clearer, upward borne,*
> *The Fairy of the Fountain rose:*
> *The halo quivering round her, grew*
> *More steadfast, as the shape shone through—*
> *O sure, a second, softer Morn*
> *The Elder Daylight knows!*

Born from the blue of those deep eyes,
Such love its happy self betray'd
As only haunts that tender race,
With flower or fount their dwelling place—
The darling of the earth and skies
She rose—that Fairy Maid!

BULWER LYTTON, "THE FAIRY BRIDE"[6]

FAIRIES AND PLANT SEX

Indeed, every act of sexual intercourse which has occurred
between those unlike one another is adultery. . . . If you
are born a human being, it is the human being who will
love you. If you become a spirit, it is the spirit which will
be joined to you. If you become thought, it is thought which
will mingle with you. If you become light, it is the light
which will share with you.

GOSPEL OF PHILIP IN JOSEPH B. LUMPKIN, *THE GNOSTIC*
GOSPELS OF PHILIP, MARY MAGDALENE, AND THOMAS

In addition to the various fairies rumored to have sexual relations with humans, many scholars have also recorded sexual relationships with nature spirits as part of indigenous shamanism. The shamans themselves, as collected in data from many places around the world, have stated that they engage in sexual relationships with certain fairylike plant spirits. The *Banisteriopsis caapi* vine, one of the ingredients of the ayahuasca brew, is one of those sexy vegetable entities. Stephan Beyer, well-known author and speaker on shamanism and spirituality, elaborates on these spirit relationships.

The Shuar tell stories of men who have sex with *tsunki* women, the shamanically potent underwater people, a manifestation of Tsunki, the primordial shaman, and get power from them; a female shaman has reported a vision of having sex with a male tsunki. Widowed or unmarried Achuar women may—although this is rare—become shamans, and maintain exclusive sexual relationships with Tsunki. Asháninka apprentice shamans suck tobacco paste until they transform into jaguars, fly through the air, and couple with the spirit of tobacco in the form of a woman, whereupon they become shamans, united with the tobacco spirit, traveling the forest as a jaguar.[7]

The shamans would establish relationships with these entities primarily to gain healing powers through them. The plants would give them information and data on which medicines to administer to sick people or would educate them on the ways of nature. The intimate nature of these relationships created some drama for many of the shamans involved as the plant spirits, much like the fairies, were known to be tricksters, not always acting in the practitioner's best interests. The theme of jealousy is apparent in many of these relationships.

There has been very little research on sexual relations between shamans and plant spirits. Certainly the spirits can be *muy celosa,* very jealous, about sexual relations between shamans and human persons. Relations with the spirits may imply both sexual abstinence with humans and sexual alliance with the spirits. There are reports of erotic ayahuasca visions; regular ayahuasca use apparently does nothing to abate—and, by report, may significantly enhance—sexual desire and performance. Psychologist Benny Shanon notes that ayahuasca drinkers "often detect a sensuous, even sexual flavor in whatever surrounds them," including the eroticization of plants and trees; he reports his own visions of semi clad women dancing erotically and lasciviously. Ethnobotanists Richard Schultes and Robert Raffauf remark, rather dryly, that "erotic aspects often reported may be due to the individual differences of the participants."[8]

Using plants as an aphrodisiac has a long history. It becomes easier to wrap the mind around the idea that plant spirits can sexually interact with humans when we realize that we use plants to assist our sexual activities all the time. The chemicals contained in many plants can stimulate and nourish the human generative organs. Herbs used to increase libido and fertility and assist in childbirth are well known throughout all cultures.

Many shamans develop relationships with these plants and their familiar spirits. They accomplish this by fasting for several days and then ingesting nothing but the plant with which they are trying to connect. They also perform meditation techniques or other rituals to coax the spirit to come visit them. Far from being a strange occurrence, this was a well-known practice in some cultures, as discussed by Mircea Eliade.

> Sexual relations between young people and spirits are quite frequent among the Yakut; they are equally frequent among a great many other peoples, without warranting any affirmation that they constitute the primary experience generating so complex a religious phenomenon as shamanism. . . . According to Sliepzova's account, if the shaman dreams of an abassy and has sexual relations with her, he wakes feeling well, certain that he will be summoned in consultation the same day and no less certain that he will be successful; if, on the contrary, he dreams that he sees the abassy full of blood and swallowing the sick person's soul, he knows that the patient will not live, and, if summoned the next day to attend him, he makes every effort to avoid the duty.[9]

SPIRITUAL SPOUSE

Love, whose month is ever May,
Spied a blossom passing fair
Playing in the wanton air:
Through the velvet leaves the wind,

All unseen 'gan passage find;
That the lover, sick to death,
Wish'd himself the heaven's breath.

WILLIAM SHAKESPEARE,
LOVE'S LABOUR'S LOST

In the majority of indigenous cultures, there are tales of shamans who interact with a spirit wife or husband who becomes so jealous he or she will not allow the shaman to have a real-life partner and works to destroy any potential relationship through their manipulations. The astral wives and husbands of the indigenous practitioners of medicine read very much like the relations between the vestals and their dominating spirits. By submitting to these kinds of relationships with spirits, the shamans gain abilities, knowledge, and healing powers. Tales of spirit spouses can be found throughout the world, and much like the fairy wife, they confer favors on their doting humans. The spirit spouse is known as an assistant and guide and sometimes even a distant ancestor of the practitioner. Most of this relationship is realized either while the shaman is in a plant-induced trance or in dreams. Entire relationships are lived out in this fashion, and the spirit spouse gains so much power over the human partner that he or she greatly influences the human's decisions.

Taking on a spirit spouse is literally the highest of attainment in alchemical and most pagan practices; however, as stated in Christian and Jewish sources, these spirits are seen as unclean—unless, of course, you are the Virgin Mary. Evangelical, Pentecostal, and other factions of Christianity actually have methods and prayers to "divorce" the familiar spirit, in essence blocking this spiritual accomplishment. In Judaism, too, even though it was recognized that many of the patriarchs received help from angels, the women who garnered the same angelic assistance were immediately put to death.

Some of the prayers to divorce your spiritual hieros gamos, or holy matrimonial familiar partner, can be found in contemporary evangelical material.

A witch causing a monster to appear before Marcomir, king of the Franks. It is her desire that draws her heavenly soul mate to appear.
Woodcut print, from Sebastian Münster, *Cosmographia Universalis* (1544)

To Overcome Spirit Husband or Spirit Wife: One of the things to overcome them is through holiness, walking in purity of the body, soul and spirit. However, the spirit husband is very strong and hard to divorce and overcome. The water spirit has variety of families, these include, the queen of the coast, python spirit, spirit spouse, spirit children. Sadly, it is almost impossible for some Christians to divorce and overcome the rage of spirit spouse in their lives. These spirits are the most formidable demons hindering many people's deliverance, victory, health, financial breakthrough, academic success, fruitfulness, etc. All over the world, the spirit husband, spirit wife, and spirit children are responsible for late marriages, marital problems, miscarriages, barrenness, long staying of pregnancy, financial debt, hardship. For example, a relationship between a married woman and the spirit spouse can cause serious setbacks, thereby making it difficult for some married women to conceive or bear children successfully.[10]

The evangelicals also view the watchers as horrible entities that can mess you up if they attach themselves to you. Most evangelical literature quotes a passage of the Bible from Paul and Silas in Acts 16 about a girl who has a familiar spirit believed to be a spy. The idea of a familiar spirit who is trying to thwart you, called a monitoring spirit, is seen in quite a lot of different sects' materials. According to the church material, the monitoring spirits, also known as familiar spirits, all belong to Satan and are like spies trying to track you and throw you off course, using information they know about you, kind of like a bad friend who betrays you by using your secret personal confessions against you.

These monitoring spirits closely resemble tales of the evil eye or the idea of someone with ill intent watching you. There is the eye of providence, which oversees things in a protective fashion, but then there is the insidious eye, like the eye of Sauron in the Lord of the Rings trilogy, which has the opposite effect. In the Yoruba tradition in Africa, this large overseeing evil eye is called the *awon aye*. This watchful malefic eye is similar to the idea of the watchers, who, as noted earlier, can be both bad and good: some watcher spirits protect you; others bring you harm. Indigenous cultures also report guardian spirits, familial spirits, and then other spirits who have ill intent, from whom your guardians protect you. Perhaps closer to reality is that we all have guardian spirits, like the fetch, and they can act either for or against ourselves and others, depending on various intentions or situations—but this is all speculation.

10

Queen Mothers and Dragon Kings in Chinese Legends

By doing nothing, the human may be united with the
Heavenly, and men may bring back their True condition.
By means of the conversations between the guardian spirit
of the Ho and Zo (the god).

F. MAX MÜLLER, *THE SACRED BOOKS OF CHINA*

I t is difficult to conceive how vast China is. For those of us living in the West, with our limited sense of history and culture, I believe it is important to look to the East before we consider anything as an original thought. It is a good practice to check to see if the Chinese have already figured it out. China has many legends of guardian spirits in all forms. Be they animal, supernatural creature, or ancestor, all the different types of familiar spirits are described in great detail throughout Chinese historical religious and spiritual literature. Perhaps the most extensive and specific material is to be found in the annals of the Taoists. Taoism, a panentheistic nature religion that spread far and wide across the East, recognized all types of familiar spirits.

The Taoist alchemists, much like the Egyptians, believed that unifying with your guardian spirit in a type of marriage was the source of all power. Just as Isis came into relationship with the angels who gave her information and data about civilization, Kuan Yin had a familiar spirit who was a dragon, in the same way the Oracle of Delphi had her Python. Most of the practices of the Taoist immortals involved varying methods to come into harmony with a guiding spirit and the spirit of nature through practices that brought things into a balance of opposing forces, or, more specifically, uniting heaven and Earth. The Taoist alchemical wedding closely resembles the union of Isis and her angels, described by Egyptian alchemists. The stories so closely follow the concept of the hieros gamos that we can see the Chinese had access to the same intelligences that presented the knowledge to Africa.

The Taoists called the shamans, sorcerers, and witches who had acquired unity with their guardian spirits the *xian,* or *hsien.* These names were interpreted in a few different fashions, the first one being of a mountain human or mountain spirit. The xian were known to practice alchemical techniques of immortality, which included relationships with the spirits of heaven, plants, and animals, as well as through psychical and meditative practices. The Taoists also called their guiding intelligences *djinn,* or genii, and these were like the genius or conscience.

Often, the xian were shown riding dragons or other creatures to

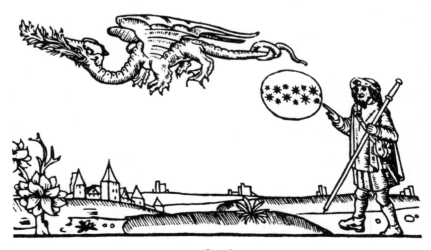

Dragon familiar spirit
Anonymous engraving, seventeenth century

symbolize their unification with their guardian familiar spirit. They were also shown with wings, much like Western depictions of angelic beings, and one of the original meanings of Taoist was said to be "feathered person." The word *xian (hsien)* can also mean "a fairy" or refer to the fairy realm. We see the direct connections between these concepts made in texts on Chinese alchemy.

> There is much in common with the traditional spirit and fairy world in the powers exhibited by the *hsien*—in their powers of invisibility, shape-shifting and flying, and in their ability to pass through solids and summon up the magic table that provides unlimited food and drink. There is also the phenomena of time-loss and timelessness, as in fairy stories, when mortals disappear for what seems a few moments or hours only to return and find a world hundreds of years older. The *hsien* Tungfang went missing for a year as a child; on being reproached by his foster-mother, he gave an account of wanderings in supernatural realms, though he insisted that he had gone out in the morning and returned at noon on the same day. . . . The idea of the *hsien* greatly appealed to the Chinese mind and there were countless stories of the Immortals or Genii.[1]

QUEEN MOTHER

> *Similar connections are found in many Ming-Qing accounts, in which the fox appears to be a subordinate of a female deity, such as the Queen Mother of the West, Guanyin, or Bixia Yuanjun, who was publicly celebrated and officially sanctioned but embodied amoral powers beyond political control and granted self-interested favors.*
>
> XIAOFEI KANG, *THE CULT OF THE FOX*

The xian, or hsien, sound very much like the fairy changelings, and their experience sounds a bit like entering the wardrobe into Narnia.

Interdimensional experiences are expounded upon at length in the Taoist literature, much like happens in tales of the Celtic fairy realms. The word *xian/hsien* can frequently be found in Taoist folktales about the fairy realms, which read quite stunningly like the Celtic versions of these stories. These folktales have a similar cast of characters, only with different names. The Taoists even had their version of the fairy queen Titania, who was known as Queen Mother. Queen Mother was a sexually seductive fox spirit woman. She inhabited the ancestor mounds and caves much like the earth goddesses of the Western European world. There were fox cults all over China who worshipped her, and they all used female spirit mediums who channeled the spirits of the dead at cemeteries and grave mounds. The fox spirits who became the human women oracles were also called ghost houses because they worked with the unclean spirits and had contact with the dead. The descriptions of these necromancers fit very closely to the practices and tales of the Oracle of Delphi and the sibyls.

> Of all the superstitions relating to spirits, those respecting a class of them called *Tu-sien* have perhaps the greatest influence upon the minds of people. *Tu-sien,* signifying a spirit in the body, designates a familiar spirit, by the assistance of which it is believed that persons are able to tell fortunes and converse with the dead. . . . They do this by dwelling in their bodies as familiar spirits, and being their medium of communication with the unseen world. Persons supposed to be possessed of these spirits are visited by multitudes, particularly those who have recently lost relatives by death. . . . Some of these fortune-tellers who have no indebted spirit to offer his services are obliged to devise means to secure the assistance of one. With this end in view, they first procure a little image made of the wood of the willow, for which they obtain a spirit in one of the following ways: Some go to a grave-yard, and after feasting the ghosts of the dead, make an arrangement with one to reside in the image. The image is then worshiped for several weeks continuously, and left out

of doors during the night, to be wet with the dews of heaven, and drink in virtue from moonbeams; after which it is regarded as an oracle, from which the spirit speaks infallibly.[2]

The word *xian* was also used for immortal animal spirits, such as familiars, the most well-known of these being the *hu xian,* or fox spirit. *Hu* in Chinese means "fox," but there were certain foxes who were more than just foxes. Tales of these foxes were legendary. A hu xian fox usually could be easily distinguished because it had more than one tail, sometimes up to nine of them. For some reason, certain animals were predisposed, more than others, to evolve and contain spiritual properties. In Asia, the fox was considered one of these animals.

In addition to its auspicious connotations in political texts, the fox was perceived as a spectral animal able to metamorphose and to bewitch people. . . . The fox assumes the roles of a shaman, a diviner, a sorcerer, and a celestial being all at once. Age played a significant role in gaining the power of metamorphosis. A long-lived creature could evolve from a lower animal level to a human being and then to a transcendent. The renowned fourth-century alchemist Ge Hong (283–343) made this point explicitly: "As for all ten thousand things that become aged, their spirits can assume human shape. . . . Foxes and wolves live to eight hundred, and at five hundred they assume human shape."[3]

The fact that these animals could change into human form is extremely interesting to me. In the West, we are very familiar with humans who can take animal form. These people are traditionally called shapeshifters, and we all know about werewolves, humans who turn into wolves. But what if, dear reader, we are confused? What if it is the wolves who are turning into humans? For some reason, we are so blinded by our anthropomorphic view that we assume it must be the other way around because animals are so low on the evolutionary chain compared to us. But in the Chinese traditions, the foxes were animal spirits who could change into humans in quite a plot twist.

> Humans and beasts are different species, but foxes are between humans and beasts. The dead and the living walk different roads, but foxes are between the dead and the living. Transcendents and monsters travel different paths, but foxes are between transcendents and monsters. Therefore, one could say to meet a fox is strange; one could also say it is ordinary. Human beings and physical objects belong to two different categories; fox-spirits stand somewhere between the two. The paths of light and darkness never converge: fox-spirits stand somewhere between the two. Immortals and demons go different ways; fox spirits stand somewhere between the two.[4]

Not only could these foxes take human form, but they could also live human lives and have human families. There are many tales of sexual relationships between humans and fox spirits, just like between humans and fairies. In Japan fox women who seduce men, known as the *kitsune,* are hugely popular. All over Japan, the kitsune are well known as shapeshifting seductresses who seduce men and make them their husbands. They were considered immortal nature spirits. In *The Cult of the Fox,* Xiaofei Kang writes that "foxes also metamorphosed into handsome men or beautiful women in order to pursue sexual relationships with humans of the opposite sex. A classic example is the story of 'Azi (the Purple),' dated to the fourth century. It recounts how a man was bewitched and taken away by a woman. When people found him, they saw his looks resembled those of a fox."[5]

Much like the fairy folk who left their bloodlines on family coats of arms in Europe, the familiar spirits left generational signatures with families all over China. There were four main animal totems in ancient China (although later many more, and some people argue that the four guardians of the directions are the main ones) that were used primarily as clan identifiers, similar to the way the Native Americans would place a totem pole outside their villages. The Chinese, too, had huge stone obelisks with their animal familiar totem mounted upon them, designating the area under their watch.

Most remarkable, however, is that another name for these fox spirits who become human, marry, and have families is the Chinese word *hu-men*. It is hard not to notice that this word, *hu-men*, bears a remarkable resemblance to the English word *human*. Though etymologically there is likely no relation between hu-men and human, it is nothing less than intriguing and suggests the close kinship between humans and natural spirits. The Chinese word or character *men* has a dual meaning: "gate" and "family." The ideogram shows a gate through which things could pass. This gate to me seems to echo the portal on Glastonbury Tor and the gate to which Cybele holds the keys, the underworld doorway that the Queen Mother guards. *Men* also means a certain kind of thinking, along the lines of "like-minded" or "kindred." The four main guardians of China are called Szu Ta Men, translated as "the four great families." In an article in *Folklore Studies,* Li Wei-tsu writes:

> The term, *szu ta-men,* literally, "The Four Great Families," is a collective name for four kinds of worshipped animals, i.e., the fox, weasel, hedgehog and snake. The belief in these four animals as sacred is very widespread amongst the rural population in the Peking area. Not all animals belonging to these four groups are regarded as sacred; the ones of a purely profane character may be hunted, the others, however, are taboo as game."[6]

Wei-tsu goes on to report that the profane animals are often quite timid, whereas the sacred ones have no fear of humans.

DRAGON KINGS

The Dragon is the most powerful . . . animal or totem living in the consciousness of the Chinese masses. The

Dragon is named as "Long" or "lung." . . . He displays both negative and positive factors. . . . He has a great strength to devastate the property, to form of floods making of the tidal waves and storms badly.

DharmaKeerthi Sri Ranjan and Zhou Chang,
"The Chinese Dragon Concept as a
Spiritual Force of the Masses"

Aside from the fox spirits and their human connections, the other prominent familiar spirit in China of epic proportions is the dragon. The dragon was considered the most powerful familiar spirit and was adopted by virtually all the emperors in Chinese history; it was thought to be of heaven and the most masculine, or yang, energy available in the animal kingdom and so the most sought-after for all the manly male emperors. To have a dragon as a familiar spirit meant that you were indeed a man of heaven, as the dragon was connoted with heaven itself. This dragon spirit is much like the spirit in Egypt who gave Hermes or Thoth the gift of language and the Python of Delphi who gave so much wisdom to all who came to hear.

In Taoist literature, such as "The Book of Divine Incantations," immortals known as the dragon kings, thought to have some of the greatest power on Earth, are mentioned. The dragon kings, the highest ranked rulers in history, achieved the highest honors and recognitions of heaven. It was said that a dragon king, a ruler who had a dragon as his familiar spirit, could control the weather and call the winds at his command. Since dragons were such powerful spirits of nature, they could command nature and in turn provide this ability to their human counterparts.

According to some sources, many Chinese people from all over China claimed that they were physically descended from dragons. A deep familiarity existed with these spirits as they were claimed to be blood relatives. The original prototypical couple in Chinese culture, equivalent to Adam and Eve, were half human and half dragon. They were called Fu Xi and Nu Wa and were responsible for bringing language and civilization to

China. Much like the ancient oracles, they also provided the divination system of the I Ching to the world after Fu Xi saw it on the back of a turtle. In true daimonic fashion, these dragon beings were also diviners, who assisted people with their decision making. In Chinese mythology, this pair generated the human race. Many Chinese still believe that they have dragon blood in their ancestry; much like the fox families and Nephilim, the dragons interbred with humans. In the article "The Chinese Dragon Concepts as a Spiritual Force of the Masses," the authors, DharmaKeerthi Sri Ranjan and Zhou Chang, write that "the homogeneous tradition has a huge network of social system and remarked the China as 'The land of Dragon' proudly and believed that the nation descended from Dragon. The biological phenomenon mingles into the social phenomenon and it triggers to articulate the ongoing history of social structure."[7]

One of the main names for these dragon spirits is *tian long*. The term *tian long* has several different meanings and interpretations, one even being a centipede, but mostly it refers to a special class of dragons who interacted with humans for their benefit. The tian long were benefactors of humans who taught them and helped them during their life on Earth. Another word used in Asia for these dragon spirits is *naga*. The naga serpents, or dragons, were known all over Asia for their ability to confer enlightenment upon a human. The nagas were probably the most sought-after familiar involved in the spiritual practices of India, Nepal, Tibet, China, and Indonesia. Special nagas, called Naga Babas, were considered ancestors, like grandfathers, who could bestow divine wisdom on humans. This idea of the Naga Baba heavily influenced the tradition of the guru in Eastern religions. To have a teacher who was wise and had worked with a dragon familiar was to become part of the Naga Baba lineage. The best example of an enlightened person with a naga are images of Buddha seated in the lap of a serpent with multiple heads. Buddha and the naga are less popular in Buddhist tradition in the West, but if you visit many parts of Asia, you will be struck by the large number of statues of Buddha seated under the great naga dragon, who is none other than the familiar spirit tian long.

11

The Rishi Families
and Guiding Guardians
of India

"Light from the East," India has given more light to the west than it has derived from that quarter. We see India in Greece in many things but not Greece in India in any. The votaries of animal magnetism, clairvoyance and so-called spiritualism will find most of their theories represented or far out done by corresponding notions existing in the yoga system for more than two thousand years.

VALMIKI, *THE YOGA-VASISHTHA
MAHARAMAYANA OF VALMIKI*

In Indian and yogic traditions, there are animal familiars, ancestors, and guiding spiritual entities. Yogis have been doing practices to access the daimonic genius and describing fairies and familiar spirits as long as all the other cultures and perhaps longer. All the versions of the familiars described in other parts of this book can also be found in India. The fairy realm described all over Europe can be found in the tales of the devas, who can be angelic and elemental spirits and also nature and animal spirits. In the Indian Vedas many otherworldly creatures who interact with human beings are described, just like in the fairy faith. "In the Semitic East, it is an old belief that a successful fast in the wilderness of forty days and nights gives power over the Djinn. The Indian *yogi* fasts till he sees face to face all the gods of the Pantheon. . . . Bread and meat would have robbed the ascetic of many an angel's visit."[1]

The Hindus are idolaters and focus devotional energy into statues of their gods and devas to invoke their powers. Many of these practices are said to yield results in the form of wishes granted, as if through the agency of a genii. Many Hindu households have a guiding genii that the family places upon a house altar in the same way the ancient Romans did. Many Hindu families hold the same guardians for generations. More generalized guardians are also sought for their particular area of expertise. When someone wants something, he or she goes to the temple and entreats the help of the specific idol in charge of whatever the devotee is trying to achieve or manifest, much like in the pagan Greek and Roman traditions. The Hindu tradition is pantheistic, recognizing a vast array of divine beings and spirits. Numerous tales of animal souls, unification with animal consciousness, guardian angels, and divine beings providing guidance can be found in the Vedic and yogic literature.

RISHI FAMILIES

We have to grow Spiritually to receive all the Knowledge the Rishis are waiting to give us.

GURUJI KRISHNANANDA

The Indians also have stories of devas, the Indian version of fallen angels and fairies, interbreeding with humans. The ancient myths of India describe *rishis,* entities very much like angels. These rishis came to Earth from the pole star in the Big Dipper. One such rishi, Angiras, is said to be one of the ancestors of the human race; he came down to

Earth to marry humans and produce offspring. The Rig-Veda hymns were composed by four families of seers, or rishis, the oldest being the Angirasas. Angiras is the primordial rishi who arises from Agni, who is sometimes conflated with a real human sage and guru. Out of this one family the other three families of seers in the Rig-Veda were derived—the Bhrigus, Kashyapas, and Atharvans. These families form the "familiar" spirit ancestors of India. Angiras also provided the humans with knowledge of civilization and valuable instruction in the ways of coming into the higher realms of being in the same way the angels conferred this on Isis and the belly-talkers of Greece. Below we see how they were thought of as teachers, or instructors, of humanity.

> Prof. Roth (in Peter's Lexicon) defines the Angirases as an intermediate race of higher beings between gods and men; while Prof. Weber, according to his invariable custom of modernising and anthropomorphising the divine, sees in them the original priests of the religion which was common to the Aryan Hindus and Persians. Roth is right. "Angirases" was one of the names of the Dhyanis, or Devas instructors ("guru-deva"), of the late Third, the Fourth, and even of the Fifth Race Initiates.[2]

Madame Blavatsky formulated her concept of the "root races" based on much of this Indian and Vedic literature outlining the bloodlines of the fallen angels who were the rishis and used it to explain the various abilities of the different races of humans. This theory later would become quite controversial as it was rumored to influence the Nazis' misguided concepts of race and hierarchy, although that had nothing to do with Madame Blavatsky's original intention or information.

GUIDING GUARDIANS

The whole idea is that these yidams must not be regarded as external gods who will save you, but they are expressions of your true nature. You identify yourself with the attributes and colors of particular yidams and feel the sound that comes from the mantra so that finally you begin to realize that your true nature is invincible. You become completely one with the yidam.

CHÖGYAM TRUNGPA, *CUTTING THROUGH SPIRITUAL MATERIALISM*

In India we can also find their version of the genius, or informing guiding spirit. All over India it is said that these spirits were responsible for guiding the Buddhas and yogis to enlightenment. This function is similar to that of other spirit guardians previously mentioned. From the Native Americans to people of the farthest reaches of Egypt, we see the pattern of strange supernatural sources educating humans. In India this spirit is called a *yidam,* a word that means "bonded" or "linked together" as in a marriage. The yidam spirit is obtained through methods similar to those used by the Native Americans, and joining with the yidam is the driving purpose behind many ascetic spiritual practices in India. Some scholars have suggested that Buddha underwent this process while sitting beneath the Bodhi Tree; he was engaging in a hieros gamos with his genius. Once united with his yidam, or daimon, Buddha began prophesying. Author John Campbell Oman describes how these spirits, also known as djinn, can confer power to the one who calls them.

Away I went in a state of nervous excitement, and, locking myself in my chamber, commanded the unseen *djinn* to bring those stones to me at once. Hardly had my mandate been uttered, when, to my amazement and secret terror, the stones lay at my feet. I went back and told the *sadhu* of my success. "Now," he said, "you have a power which you can exercise over everything upon which you can make the mystical sign I have taught you, but use your power with discretion, for my gift is qualified by the fact that, do what you will, the things, whatever they may be, acquired through your *familiar* spirit, cannot be accumulated by you, but must soon pass out of your hands." And the *sadhu's* words have been verified in my life, and his gift has not been an unmixed blessing, for my *djinn* resents my power, and has often tried to harm me; but happily his time is not yet come.[3]

In addition to attracting a yidam with which to perform the hieros gamos, the yogis were able to become disembodied like these spirits. The technique to become a spirit, free of the body, was known as transference. Transference of consciousness is a technique that yogis in India have practiced for thousands of years. Kind of like the Greek belly-talkers who throw their voice into someone's mind, the yogi throws his or her awareness or consciousness into the body of another living thing. It is said that this superpower was given to certain lineages directly through the devas and rishis themselves. In his book *The Deva Handbook: How to Work with Nature's Subtle Energies,* Nathaniel Altman writes, "Devas can be defined as forms, images, or expressions through which the essences and energy forces of the Creator or Great Spirit can be transmitted, or forms through which a specific form of Earth energy or life force can be transmitted for a specific purpose."[4]

This transference of consciousness is mentioned in many of the ancient yogic texts, including the Yoga Sutras of Patanjali. Here it is mentioned that one can throw the consciousness into animals, nature, and other humans. Some yogis were reputed to live through another person's body using this technique and operate that person as if he or she were a puppet. Many tales of these kinds of activities are articulated in a great volume called *Sinister Yogis* by David Gordon White.

As strange as it may sound, currently several groups are attempting to do this with technology by transferring their consciousness into machines and computers, a technique called mind uploading. Several scientists at MIT are very serious about this research. This transference of memories into a computer represents an extreme idolization of the human mind. In Tibet, this ability is called *phowa;* in this practice

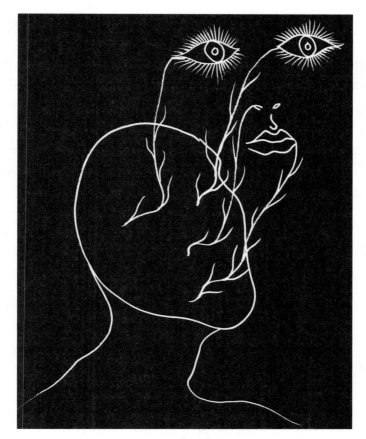

Transference
Original art by Maja D'Aoust

the individual throws his or her consciousness free from the body right before death. Phowa practice involves dream techniques and intense meditations to prepare the consciousness to depart the physical body and arrive at another location. This superpower was affiliated with the guru teachings.

This concept of the transference of consciousness or energy would, years later, influence Franz Anton Mesmer, a German physician who cured patients of hysteria, pain, and other maladies using techniques he developed based on a theory he called animal magnetism. His theory was essentially the very same Indian practice of energy transference given as a power from the familiars. The theory spread widely and was used extensively, becoming extremely popular. One of its most efficacious uses for years was to provide a kind of anesthesia for people undergoing surgery. Shockingly, the Mesmer techniques using Indian energy transference and artificial somnambulism, a type of hypnosis, successfully allowed people to have surgery without anesthesia up until the discovery of ether. In 1843 animal magnetism evolved into the practice of hypnotism as we know it today, which is practiced widely all over the globe and has its roots in an ancient Indian psychic technique gained from the guru rishis.

12
The Voices in Our Heads

<div align="center">~~~</div>

The Daimon, the Genius, and the Double

Socrates' daimon *was not some "inner voice," but an external sign or command that would suddenly cause him to stop in his tracks.*

SIMON CRITCHLEY, *THE BOOK OF DEAD PHILOSOPHERS*

The role of the guardian is explored in great detail in the daimonic literature. Here we find a very practical way that familiar spirits serve humans. A bit different from the oracle, the daimon and genius offer information in the form of guidance and warnings, issued when needed most. The relationship between a human and his guiding intelligence is interpreted in several Greek and magical sources and differs slightly from the traditional witch who might use a familiar for divination.

THE GENIUS AND THE DAIMON

Only the Genius knows, who goes with us and moderates our natal star, that God of human birth, who dies with each of us.

HORACE

There is a special form that a familiar spirit can take; it is one that might not be expected. A familiar spirit can exist only within the mind of a human and speak through that human. This voice is experienced as very real and gives specific commands that are usually particular to the events happening in the moment. It is guiding and instructional.

We are told not to talk to ourselves or listen to the voices in our heads. But thankfully, there are many who ignore these proscriptions

Best friend, guardian daimon
Original art by Maja D'Aoust

and follow their intuition to listen to the guidance system inside their head. Not everyone experiences such a phenomenon, and those who do hear voices are usually diagnosed with a mental illness. This stigma and taboo against internal dialogue within the mind has driven all the individuals who experience such things into isolation. They dare not tell anyone of their experiences for fear of being committed to a mental ward. People experiencing this become alienated because something is happening to their mind that most others do not experience and that is looked upon as dangerous. This could not have been more different in ancient times. If an individual heard a voice, it was often thought that he or she was gifted. It was an omen that this person had a calling to the priesthood or the college of diviners.

The Christian church often identified the voice as Satan, also known as the adversary or the deceiver. Most who claimed to hear the voice of God were called heretics and put to death. It was certainly not acceptable to claim that guidance was coming directly from God or a higher spirit: this was reserved for the biblical patriarchs or Jesus Christ alone. On the other hand, the church had much literature about guardian angels and spirits who watched over people. It was acceptable to hear an angel, conscience, or the Holy Ghost or spirit speaking and offering guidance.

The Bible is rife with stories of individuals hearing the voice of God. Noah, for example, heard a voice that gave him very detailed instructions for building the ark and saving his family. But can we really separate this voice of God that Noah heard, instructing him on how to build a seaworthy vessel, from, say, the instructions Nikola Tesla received for building an alternating current device, which he reported happened to him while he was out for a leisurely stroll one day? The pagans viewed all of the voices, whether conscience, guiding intellect, or genius, as a collective whole that had different faces, like the facets on a diamond. Many of the great thinkers, inventors, and geniuses of humanity have reported hearing such a voice and felt compelled to follow its commands.

One such individual who claimed to hear this voice very clearly and stated that the voice informed many of his choices and intelligence was Socrates. There was a long tradition of this in Greece among the philosophers, and they called these helpful presences the daimons, which is where we get our modern word *demon*. In the end, poor Socrates met his death due in part to his claims that he had this special friend, informing and guiding him, despite the fact that the things he said were usually exactly correct and very wise.

> Athena's famous appearances to Achilles, Diomedes and Telemachus in the *Iliad* and *Odyssey* are thus reformulated as epic examples of a widespread phenomenon that also embraces oracles, ghosts and the personal *daimonion* of Socrates, which Maximus' oration on *daimones* seeks to normalize through the enumeration of epiphanic *comparanda*. In this, he takes his lead from Diotima's speech in Plato's *Symposium*: "Everything that is daemonic is intermediate between God and mortal . . . Interpreting and transporting human things to the gods and divine things to men, and ordinances and requitals from above: being midway between, it makes each to supplement the other, so that the whole is combined in one . . . God has no contact with men; but the daemonic is the means of all society and converse of gods with men and of men with gods, whether waking or asleep. Whosoever has skill in these affairs is a daemonic man."[1]

The daimon of the Oracle of Delphi liked the daimon of Socrates so much she decreed that "no one was wiser than Socrates." Ironically, this decree may have sealed his fate: others were jealous of his fame and wanted this recognition for themselves. Socrates was merely sharing the truths he learned through his daimon, but he was viewed as a heretic who placed himself in a higher position than others. For how could Socrates be so favored by the gods that he would receive communication and others not be able to do so? Socrates taught in depth how to achieve contact with this conscience for others as well; however, such instructions were heeded only by his closest students, who had to watch in horror as he was put to death. They moaned and wept through the experience and could not contain their grief and emotion. But Socrates remained calm and collected and even berated them for carrying on like a bunch of women. The price to pay for letting others know about your familiar spirit was severe and a matter of life and death.

The difficult part of the genii, or daimon, is that it seems to be two sided or have a dual nature, as if there are two different advocates having an argument within the human mind. It can be both helpful and destructive, guiding one to greatness or ruin, according to most people who have described such an experience. The dual nature of the inner voice has given rise to the popular image of an angel and a devil, each perched on a shoulder, whispering things in a person's ears. The negative aspect of the voice has been called the adversary, or deceiver, and it seems to argue against doing something rather than supporting an action. Socrates said that his daimon only told him when not to do something, as in a warning.

A friend once told me of an experience she had with a guiding voice. She had just been talking about St. Francis and then went to get in her car. Along the way she passed an old woman who was holding a postcard with a picture of St. Francis on it. The woman was standing on a curb staring out into space. A voice in my friend's head said, commandingly, "Give her a ride!" She chose to ignore it and went her way. Though an individual may receive guidance, ultimately it's up to him or her to decide what to do.

The daimons were specifically tied to decision making and were thought to be guides or tutors to help the person make the best decision possible. This was also the purpose of divination and what the oracles and witches were used for, to provide information that could assist with decision making. As a professional witch, this is how every session with my clients is spent, attempting to arrive at a best possible decision. Daimons had to do with divination, specifically, and fortunes, rather like the association of the word *fairy* with "fate." The root of *daimon* is *da,* meaning "to divide," as in the division of lots or fates.

Guardian
Original art by Maja D'Aoust

demon. c. 1200, from Latin daemon "spirit," from Greek daimon "deity, divine power; lesser god; guiding spirit, tutelary deity" (sometimes including souls of the dead); "one's genius, lot, or fortune"; from PIE *dai-mon- "divider, provider" (of fortunes or destinies), from root *da- "to divide."[2]

Here we see that *daimon* has rather the same meaning as *fairy* and is related to fate and fortune. The genius is a guide to our destiny and our "lot" in life, and so it is closely related to the fairy realm and the Fates.

To the chagrin of many scientists, I am afraid I need to report that the man credited with the creation of the scientific method did so using his familiar genius spirit. This very irrational pagan technique is used today by scientists all over the globe. A gentleman by the name of René Descartes spent a lot of time engaged in argument with his genius, whom he called an evil demon, or the Evil Genius Doubt, through whose agency he was able to deduce and articulate the method to determine the truth of something. The Evil Genius Doubt of Descartes was the very same adversary or deceiver described for hundreds of years by so many other religious and spiritual institutions. There is a well-known scene in the biblical apocryphal literature of Adam having an argument with Satan in the Garden of Eden.

In obscure Jewish texts, it was said that to win the ability to name the animals and have control and dominion over nature, Adam had to first match wits with the devil. They had an argument and Adam won, so he got to name the animals. There is also a scene in the New Testament that involves Jesus arguing with Satan in the desert in much the same manner. In this technique for gaining insight, the genius provides you with an adversary to go up against. Descartes used this method to "come to a decision" of truth through a process of elimination or negation. The philosopher Karl Popper went into great detail about this method as well. The way that Descartes engaged his daimon is well documented in his journals, and one who is savvy as to Socrates's daimonic methods can easily see that Descartes was using this very same occult technique to arrive at his truth. So, you see, it was in fact a divination technique that produced the scientific method. In addition, Descartes claimed to have a dream that delivered the method to his mind in its totality, resulting in the modern-day method used in every laboratory. Not a very scientific way to arrive at the scientific method, but I guess most modern scientists are more than willing to overlook this small discrepancy as they pooh-pooh all the oracles, who are in a way the mothers of their occupation.

THE HOLY GUARDIAN ANGEL
OF ALEISTER CROWLEY

The Holy Guardian Angel is the spiritual Sun of the Soul of the Adept.

ALEISTER CROWLEY

The occult group the Golden Dawn had detailed instructions for how to come into contact and union with your genius. Most of the works that discuss the inner practices of this initially closed group go into these methods. One of the early members of the Golden Dawn not only practiced these techniques but also published them without the group knowing and was kicked out as a result: that member was Aleister Crowley. Crowley, in his later works, called the daimon the Holy Guardian Angel, or HGA for short. The HGA was the exact same as the daimon and genius, and much of Crowley's work on this subject was borrowed either from the Golden Dawn or from other kabbalistic and Egyptian hermetic texts.

In his work, Crowley was very insistent that making the connection to the HGA was the most important thing for a magician to accomplish, for no other operation would hold any weight until the initiate had completed this task and become whole through the hieros gamos. The source text that the Golden Dawn group consulted was said to be a Jewish book attributed to a kabbalist named Abrehmalin the Mage. Of course, some believe this was just another name for Abraham. Could it be that this technique was similar to that given to the children of the east and that the Golden Dawn had found a way to contact the very same angels with whom Isis and the oracles had connected? From Crowley's descriptions of them, it is hard to deny the similarities. The HGA of Crowley is a daimon, just like the daimon of Socrates, Descartes, and the Oracle of Delphi. The spirits of these works are familiar, indeed.

According to Crowley, once the initiate had accomplished union

Emblem XLII: Man being led through the world
by his guardian daimon
Copperplate engraving by Matthäus Merian, from Michael Maier,
Atalanta Fugiens (1617)

with his or her familiar spirit, the initiate would be able to have a connection to heaven, and therefore, many other techniques were unneces-
sary as all one needed to do was follow the guidance of the spirit. This
might sound easy, but in fact, for human beings to follow divine guidance can prove exceedingly difficult. Just as Adam and Eve were unable
to follow the advice of God in the Garden of Eden and broke the rules,
many humans have a hard time following the advice of their guardian
spirit. Sometimes the guardian wants us to do really scary things, or
things we don't want to do, like quit drinking or become responsible.
These can be difficult instructions to act upon, and some people aban-
don the advice in favor of continuing their life as they see fit. Imagine
the case of Abraham, where this is taken to the extreme; his guiding
spirit told him to do perhaps the worst thing imaginable, kill his own

son. The strange relationships between familiar spirits and their spouses are not always pleasant, and not everyone gets a kind guardian. Some familiars are horrific and cruel as well as benevolent.

To successfully follow the techniques suggested in the works of the Golden Dawn and form a relationship with your guardian spirit, you must be able to surrender, to allow something else to guide you. This takes quite a bit of humility, and not everyone can do it. British occultist Aleister Crowley advises:

> It should never be forgotten for a single moment that the central and essential work of the Magician is the attainment of the Knowledge and Conversation of the Holy Guardian Angel. Once he has achieved this he must of course be left entirely in the hands of that Angel, who can be invariably and inevitably relied upon to lead him to the further great step—crossing of the Abyss and the attainment of the grade of Master of the Temple.[3]

Guardian spirit leading mundane animal
Anonymous etching, from Daniel Stolcius von Stolcenberg,
Viridarium Chymicum (Frankfurt, 1624)

THE GENIUS AND FAMILY ANCESTORS

Sometimes the Kore- and mother-figures slither down altogether to the animal kingdom, the favourite representatives then being the cat *or the* snake *or the* bear, *or else some black monster of the underworld like the crocodile, or other salamander-like, saurian creatures.*

CARL JUNG, *PART 1: ARCHETYPES AND THE COLLECTIVE UNCONSCIOUS*

The word *genius* means a few different things. It is mostly described as an inborn intellectual gift. It is also related to the word *gene,* like family, ancestry or even a bloodline, or genetic ability. Some have interpreted the genius as a kind of family gene in the DNA.

> **gene-** It is the hypothetical source of/evidence for its existence is provided by: Sanskrit *janati* "begets, bears," *janah* "offspring, child, person," *janman-* "birth, origin," *jatah* "born"; Avestan *zizanenti* "they bear"; Greek *gignesthai* "to become, happen," *genos* "race, kind," *gonos* "birth, offspring, stock"; Latin *gignere* "to beget," *gnasci* "to be born," gensu (genitive *generis*) "race, stock, kind; family, birth, descent, origin," *genius* "procreative divinity, inborn tutelary spirit, innate quality," *ingenium* "inborn character," possibly *germen* "shoot, bud, embryo, germ"; Lithuanian *gentis* "kinsmen"; Gothic *kuni* "race"; Armenian *chanim* "I bear, I am born."[4]

Here we see the role of the genii, genius, or daimon as a specific spirit who is somehow perhaps in our genes, blood, or DNA. The family spirit could be providing a kind of grandfatherly advice through genetic memory to the ears of those who are open enough to listen to it.

In ancient Roman culture, the genius was a house spirit and a family spirit or ancestor. In Rome they were considered family totem spirits and viewed as the lords of the houses. The Romans too viewed these spirits as generative, and as such they were also fertility gods. Many view Juno, the goddess of marriage, among other roles, as the mother of the "genius" spirits. She is associated with Vesta, her sister, the goddess of the hearth, home, and family. Vesta became the main goddess worshipped by the vestal virgins. So there was an original generative, or ancestral couple, Jupiter and Juno, like Adam and Eve, who were the most highly venerated of the familiar spirits and seen as the archetypal mother and father spirits. They were also considered marriage spirits and were in charge of matrimony. Couples who wished to get married sought them out to bless them and bless their house. In Rome and Greece, the daimon was often depicted as a serpent or snake, which echoes the ancient traditions of the Oracle of Delphi and the Python.

Serpent mother
Original art by Maja D'Aoust

The guiding genius was seen by some as given to all humans and not restricted only to those who called upon them or formed a relationship with them.

> The Etruscans believed that every human being had a protecting genius who was his constant companion, guard, and guide, both in the present world and in the realm of immortality. The Lemures were the spirits of the dead. The Lares were the spirits of virtuous ancestors who presided over the hearths and homes of their children. The Lar Familiaris was the lord of the whole family. The Larvae were the spirits of wicked ancestors, and are banished from the domestic hearth. The Manes were the souls of the departed . . . the souls of men being supposed to have emanated from that planet.
>
> The genii of the Romans were the offspring of the great gods and the givers of life itself, and hence they were called Dii Genitales. These genii received worship among the Romans as among the Etruscans. The majority of the Etruscan Genii were females, and are sometimes called *geniæ*. It is sometimes difficult to distinguish them from Fates or Furies.[5]

The progenitors, or parents, were the keepers of the genes in a very literal sense, passing along DNA and genetic information. The relation of genies and genes is quite fascinating. Our forefathers are literally stored within our genes and expressed in both behaviors and physical traits. The grandfathers in our blood are called atavisms. The word *atavism* comes to us from the Latin *atavus,* which means, literally, "a great-grandfather's grandfather." An atavism is used to describe an evolutionary throwback; namely, a genetic trait that spontaneously reappears that had disappeared generations ago. This means that things left behind by our great-great-grandparents can suddenly reappear outwardly through us, if the right trigger is provided. The most recent evidence of these phenomena was a dolphin captured off the coast of Wakayama, Japan, who had an extra pair of flippers. Atavisms are possible because all previously existing phenotypical data is stored within the DNA, even though most of these genes are not expressed in the current physical manifestation of the organism. If atavisms exist, if we can spontaneously revert back to older forms, then these forms exist within us all the time, latent though they may be. More important than these forms simply existing within us is that they contain a history of our existence in the form of data dating back at least to the creation of the DNA molecule on planet Earth. As the scholarly mystic A. E. Waite wrote, "As concerns the matter, it is *one* and contains within itself all that is needed."[6]

The fact that these atavisms can appear and disappear at will leads us to an important discovery concerning the nature of DNA and how it operates. It seems that genes can be activated and inactivated in a living organism during its own lifetime. In a single generation, we may reprogram our DNA by activating some genes and deactivating others. There has been an entire field dedicated to studying this phenomenon in recent times that has been termed *evolutionary developmental biology,* or evo-devo. Many of us tend to view our DNA as a static component of our body. It most definitely is not. While we are born with the same set of genes we will pass on to our offspring and die with, it is the modulation of gene expression that regulates our growth and response to outside stimuli, including emotions and behavior. Our genes are designed to be switched on and off without changing their composition. It is this ability that allows evolution to take place.

This dormant potentiality has much larger implications, though, than simply healing a disease. It is this latent potentiality that can determine the form of an entire organism, like whether you turn out to be a pig or a person. There is a cash pile of latent genes that have been around for quite some time and are shared by nearly every organism on the planet.

All animals have *Hox* genes, and nearly all animals use their *Hox* genes to determine which appendage should go where along the axis that runs from head to tail. . . . *Hox* genes must be at least half a billion years old. . . . Carroll calls these the "tool kit" genes. . . . Nearly all tool-kit genes are present in all animals, and they do much the same thing in all animals. The same gene, for example, that triggers eye development in fruit flies also triggers eye development in mice. Indeed, genetically engineered flies will happily build eyes if supplied only with the mouse gene. (They build fly eyes, not mouse eyes.) . . . This surprising genetic conservatism across nearly all animals is evo devo's key empirical finding: swans, swallowtails, and socialites are all built from the same genes.[7]

The existence of these cross special genetic similarities is not a new idea restricted to evo-devo; scientists have known of this phenomenon for several hundred years. It began when some scientists noticed that all embryos seem to start out the same. A German fellow named Ernst Haeckel, a contemporary of Darwin, developed his theory of recapitulation based on his observations of this in 1866. Also called the biogenetic law, embryological parallelism, or ontogeny recapitulates phylogeny, this theory offers an explanation for why apparent similarities between humans and other animals are found on these fundamental levels. Many scientists over the years have disregarded the theory as antiquated and preposterous; however, evidence discovered in the evo-devo field and atavistic discoveries have made this concept more attractive in recent times. It has not been lost on some scientists that the process of our evolving from zygote to human mirrors evolution. Further, this process suggests that our bodies contain the *memory* of evolution. That means that what we think of as our ancestors could possibly extend to all life on Earth that has DNA. That would certainly include all the animals, to say the least. So many of the tales of the familiar spirits and animal totems could simply be humans remembering and gaining access to their genes and their DNA.

ANNA KINGSFORD AND
THE ALCHEMICAL WEDDING

For the Divine Spirit of a man is not one with his soul until regeneration, which is the intimate union constituting what, mystically, is called the "marriage of the hierophant." When this union takes place, there is no longer need of an initiator; for then the office of the genius is ended. For, as the moon, Isis, or "Mother," of the planet man, the genius reflects to the soul the Divine Spirit, with which she is not yet fully united. In all things is order. Wherefore, as with the planets, so with the microcosm. . . . The prophet is a man illumined by his angel. The Christ is a man married to the Spirit. And he returns out of pure love to redeem, needing no more to return to the flesh for his own sake. Wherefore he is said to come down.

ANNA KINGSFORD,
CLOTHED WITH THE SUN

One of my favorite familiar workers is a somewhat obscure figure in the worlds of alchemy and occultism: Anna Kingsford. I synchronistically came across her work several times during my researches into alchemy, but it wasn't until I was working with Kelvin DeWolfe that my familiar spirit brought me into full accord with her practices of work with the genius, or daimon. It was directly after I had done one of the yearly spirit workings at the solstice, which involve fasting and not sleeping for five days, that I had a crystal-clear vision of the nature of the guiding spirit. After this vision, DeWolfe described his experience, which was also the same as what Kingsford discussed. Because both experiences had the same elements, it seemed to me to be true, or impossibly coincidental. I saw an image of the moon, reflecting the light of the sun and circling Earth—only I was Earth, my genius was the moon, and the sun was the light of God. Nearly instantly after receiving this message,

DeWolfe told me that he had had a similar experience, physically seeing an orb of light circling him.

After that experience I randomly came across the following work by Kingsford.

> The genius of a man is his satellite. Man is a planet. God—the God of the man—is his sun, and the moon of this planet is Isis, its initiator, or genius. The genius is made to minister to the man, and to give him light. But the light he gives is from God, and not of himself. He is not a planet but a moon, and his function is to light up the dark places of his planet. The day and night of the microcosm, man, are its positive and passive, or projective and reflective states. In the projective state, we seek actively outwards; we aspire and will forcibly; we hold active communion with the God without. In the reflective state we look inwards, we commune with our own heart; we in draw and concentrate ourselves secretly and interiorly. During this condition, the "Moon" enlightens our hidden chamber with her torch, and shows us ourselves in our interior recess. Who or what, then, is this moon? It is part of ourselves, and revolves with us. It is our celestial affinity,—of whose order is it said, "Their angels do always behold the face of My Father."[8]

This was the moment when I came into a deep realization of the true meaning of the alchemical statement of the unification of the sun and moon and the role that Earth plays in this scenario. Most folks who study alchemy come across, at some point in their research, the concept of the alchemical wedding. Also known as the alchemical marriage or *mysterium conjunctio,* at this stage of the alchemical process, the soul and spirit unify as one thing. A similar concept is expressed and practiced in hatha yoga: *yoga* means "to yoke or unite" while *ha* means "sun" and *tha* means "moon"—the joining of sun and moon. This joining sounds very mysterious and symbolic to those who have never had an encounter with their satellite or an awareness of it at all. In my opinion, everyone has a satellite, but only some are united with it, or linked to it. This was similar to DeWolfe's explanation of it as well. When you join with the satellite, as Kingsford describes so well above, you appear to have a halo of light surrounding you as you shine with the light of the sun with which you have established a relationship. For better or worse, till death do you part, your own personal satellite is there with you; it's up to you how much you come into communion with it. Much in the same way a married couple may fight or come into polarity with each other, so too you can come into polarity with your spirit. Alchemy essentially provides techniques for coming into this relationship. Kingsford described the satellite as a genius or damion.

> Every human spirit-soul has attached to him a genius or daimon, as with Socrates; a ministering spirit, as with the apostles; or an angel, as with Jesus. All these are but different names for the same thing. My genius says that he does not care for the term *angel* because it is misinterpreted. He prefers the Christian nomenclature, and to be called minister, as their office is to guide, admonish, and illumine. He tells me to say that the best weapon against the astrals is prayer. Prayer means the intense direction of the will and desire towards the Highest; an unchanging intent to know nothing but the Highest. So long as Moses held up his hands towards heaven, the Israelites prevailed. When he dropped them, then the Amalekites. The genii are not fighting spirits, and cannot prevent evils. They were allowed to minister to Jesus only after his exhaustion in combat with the lower spirits. Only they are attacked by these, who are worth attacking.[9]

Many aspects of Kingsford's life were similar to the habits of the belly-talkers and the oracles of old. She naturally gravitated to some of their preferences: isolation, preferring the company of animals, and celibacy.

In a vision in January of 1881, Kingsford's personal genius introduced her to the shade of William Lilly (a 17th-century astrologer and friend of Elias Ashmole), who interpreted her nativity. He told her that the stars had marked her out for a single career in which she could enjoy wealth and success. "The course is, however, an evil one. It is the career of the Harlot." He told her that she had begun to bring ruin on herself by marrying, and that by becoming a mother, she had closed herself off to the benefits of her stars. He forecast misfortune for her as long as she should "persist in a virtuous course of life; and, indeed, it is now too late to adopt another." . . . Idealistic and judgmental towards men and women, her affections were largely directed towards animals. She constantly kept a guinea pig as a pet, usually carrying it with her even in public . . . but the remainder of her marriage appears to have been non-sexual in its basis, and she was purportedly sexually abstinent for the rest of her life. In 1870 she converted to Roman Catholicism, receiving the name Mary at her confirmation.[10]

Kingsford mirrored fairly closely the life of the oracles with the exception of having a child and marrying, yet she still took up her prophetic office and has channeled several works on the gospels, the Bible, and Jesus Christ, which she is said to have received through the agency of her genius. Her writings and lectures were her expression of her genius, and she was able to earn her living by transmitting its messages.

In the quote above you may have noticed a curious phrase: "career of the Harlot." Many assume that this means prostitution, but this phrase is nothing less than a reference to the holy practice of the vestal virgins. When we look into the etymology of the word *harlot*, it is actually closer in meaning to a gypsy or a traveler. The harlot was on the move, a vagabond. The negative connotations associated with this word have mostly to do with racist and inappropriate views of the gypsies or Romani people because they were wrongly considered homeless vagrants and thieves. The harlot was thought to be a dirty thing with no job, or steady way to earn income, when in fact these women were usually fortune-tellers, artists, performers, and musicians. But even if they did earn their income through prostitution, this is not a reason to disparage the harlot.

On a deeper level, a harlot was a priestess of Hathor, as noted in chapter 4. Hathor, the Egyptian cow goddess, is the equivalent of Aphrodite, the Greek goddess of love, so this may have further contributed to the sexual stigmatization of these women. Priestesses of Hathor were much like the vestal virgins and belly-talkers. Providing people with prophecies and fates, they observed certain practices and customs. It is here that the career of the harlot is that of a diviner.

It is my opinion that this association of harlot with the oracles constitutes the true meaning of the Whore of Babylon in the Book of Revelation. The Whore of Babylon is none other than the forgotten high priestess who served as Pythia and served the goddess Cybele. In the Book of Revelation, the "Whore" of Babylon comes riding in on a lion, reminiscent of Cybele and her guardian lions.

People have horribly mistranslated the Hebrew word *zanah,* it seems. In the Book of Revelation, it is the *Harlot* of Babylon—the harlot who is connected to Hathor and the Creator Goddess of Earth. That the Lady of Babylon should be so misconstrued emphasizes the role Babylon plays in all our language confusion concerning the ancient myths.

The literal meaning of the word *zanah* is "to cover or place a veil over one's face," and so it suggests something shameful or to be ashamed, akin to hiding in shame, like covering the face with the hands. But if we look just a bit deeper into the significance of someone who covers up in shame, we are taken back to Genesis. Here Adam and Eve, after eating the apple, are ashamed and hide from God because they did not obey his command. They also for the first time are aware that they are naked and cover themselves. And so they begin to think of themselves as shameful. God, however, seems more upset that they are ashamed than that they disobeyed. Of course, that is a huge topic for debate; I am merely offering my opinion. To me it seemed that God was trying to convey that there was no reason for them to hide in shame because that was an illusion. In fact, in most of the depictions of God in the Hebraic texts, the face of God is covered. Humans are not permitted or cannot look upon the face of God directly; this is stated in several places in the Old Testament. To cover the face with the veil somehow meant to be shameful and shameless at the same time. How could the Harlot of Babylon be made to feel shame for the veil upon her face when God wore the same costume? The vestal virgins were often depicted with veils covering their faces, so it could be possible that the reference to the veil of the Harlot of Babylon was similar to the vestal virgins' veils and was nothing to be ashamed of.

When Anna Kingsford was told that she could have the career of the harlot, it meant that she could travel and tell fortunes, talking through her familiar genius spirit, much like a priestess giving mass. That is the true meaning of the career of the harlot. Having said that, I would also offer that being a whore does not mean that you could not be a harlot. Although most harlots choose to be celibate so as to come into union with their guiding spirits, it is not a necessary component. I am not making judgments against sex workers in these statements either; I'm simply correcting a translation error and a common misconception. There are some who are of the opinion that in ancient times the priestesses of Cybele were promiscuous and would hold huge orgies, so that may have contributed to the affiliation as well. The point is that modern folk who think that these types of female practitioners were prostitutes could not be further from the truth; they were priestesses.

Kingsford was a harlot priestess who performed the alchemical marriage of opposites with her guiding daimon spirit, and through it she was able to write and prophesy on the mysteries. She is a fabulous example of a living witch who practiced the ancient familiar magic.

THE DOUBLE

An isolated, confused, double self, a self able to speak therefore only to itself. A self arguing itself into reasons

why that self must remain isolated, confused, double self.
A paradoxical self, therefore, because it sustains a logical
discussion with itself, arguing itself into what can only be
considered, so it feels by others as madness.

PIERS GREY ON T. S. ELIOT'S POEM
"THE LOVE SONG OF J. ALFRED PRUFROCK"

In Europe, the familiar spirit was sometimes described as a double of the person, almost a copy but slightly different. The German term for this concept, *doppelgänger*, is familiar to most people, and the double has appeared in popular culture through works of fiction and film. Also called the aetheric double, this familiar double can encompass a few different things. Some sources consider it a lifelong companion, rather like a soul mate, while others describe it as a ghostly apparition that is revealed later in life, or only during a specific destiny-laden incident, such as a death. Others imagine this copy existing in a parallel reality, like Bizarro and Superman. The double can also play the role of the adversary, much like Descartes used it, as the doubter or negator.

The double has been explored by some of the greatest artistic and philosophical minds of the ages, and many claim to have had a direct experience with it. In the film *Orpheus* (*Orphée* in French), director Jean Cocteau constructs a mirror world in which the main character becomes a double, or doppelgänger, who has to traverse the spirit world. The book *Through the Looking Glass* by Lewis Carroll tells the story of Alice's adventures in a mirror world, a kind of parallel universe that her double inhabits. In many tales, the fairy realm can be entered through a mirror. The idea that we can mirror ourselves and others is a huge psychological reality for both psychology and biology.

Many things in nature mimic each other, and when we reflect upon things, including ourselves, we become strange mirrors of the things that we reflect upon. I had an overwhelming personal experience of this while contemplating the idea of the double when I was out taking a stroll. I was walking home as the sun was setting, and suddenly,

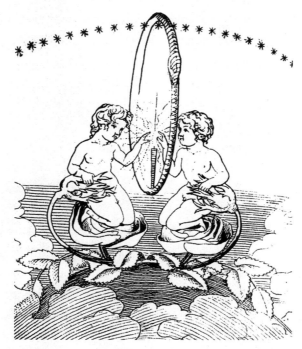

Zwei Kinder in Rosenblüten durch den Schlangengürtel
der Ewigkeit getrennt *(two children in rose flowers mirroring
each other, separated by the snake ring of eternity)*
Copperplate engraving by Philipp Otto Runge (1803)

a dove flew through a beautiful sunbeam, arcing as it approached, and landed in a very specific manner. It was so pretty that I paid very close attention to it. And then, directly after, within seconds, another dove came and mimicked exactly each and every one of the previous dove's movements as it too landed precisely next to the first dove. I felt as if I had just experienced a glitch in the matrix. It was as if a duplicate or clone of the first dove had appeared, mirroring and repeating the exact movements of the first one, or the two doves were one creature, mirror images of each other.

The mirroring of our self onto the loved one to make it something more familiar and less strange is one of the fundamental concepts of the driving force of attraction: "The true object, omnipresent of Eros, is the phantasm, which has taken permanent possession of the spiritual mirror. Now, this phantasm represents a perceived image that has gone beyond the threshold of consciousness. . . . In that way, the soul of the lover becomes the mirror in which the image of the loved one is reflected"[11] Whether or not this double is an external soul mate or some kind of version of our self that is repeated through phantasmagorical projection becomes quite the existential dilemma in philosophical terms. Can the soul mate be realized in a true outer form that becomes our mate, or are we all only projecting the hope that our own soul will come to us to become whole at last?

According to poets like T. S. Eliot and Percy Bysshe Shelley, this double is a shadow self that becomes realized when one becomes self-actualized. The self-actualization process has the effect of isolating us from others, and so we develop a kind of imaginary friend because no one else can understand what we are going through. We make our own version of our ideal self and develop such a close relationship with it that it becomes real. There were several stories of other people physically seeing the double of Percy Bysshe Shelley, including his claims that he saw it himself, especially when he, or someone close to him, became ill. This would make the double a little more complicated than just something that exists in our own subconscious mind or a projection because other people can see it too. This is where madness turns into a miraculous phenomenon, when an inner experience physically manifests. Through the double or shadow, our deepest inner self may be projected into the outer world in a way that others can see it, even if we can't see it ourselves. Several other famous figures in history experienced other people seeing their double, so Shelley's double was not an isolated incident. Goethe, the author of *Faust,* wrote about his experiences with this in detail.

The shadow self can become like an adversary or deceiver. The double is our exact opposite who is also us. Some people feel that this is what Lucifer really symbolizes, the shadow part of ourselves that lives within us but goes unnoticed most of the time. The well-known theosophist Rudolph Steiner wrote on this subject and how our Luciferian double performs a vital function in our development; namely, that of providing friction to force us to grow. We are contradictory creatures, sometimes this thing and sometimes that thing. Once a human becomes aware of their contradictions, they become more accepting of a larger part of themselves that they may not have taken into account before.

> In addition to this there is the misunderstanding which arises because, owing to the contradictory nature of the Ahrimanic and the Luciferic, wrong inferences are drawn concerning the behavior of these impulses towards the nature of man. People think—many only pretend to think—that by consciously opposing by supersensible cognition the Ahrimanic character of a mere natural knowledge, man must be led into the Luciferic. Whoever maintains this, lacks the understanding that the supersensible knowledge which man develops out of his own innermost being cannot only never lead into the Luciferic element, but directly prevents such a downfall, which would inevitably take place if a one-sided Ahrimanic impulse usurped the place of consciousness. For this would deliver over to the Luciferic the strivings after the supersensible which are not seized by man's own being. With these indications we have pointed out the obstacles which oppose man's turning towards supersensible cognition. These arise from a certain self-deception and intentional, or half-intentional, misunderstanding of human nature. If attention is directed to these obstacles by a calm and collected soul life, the possibility of such cognition will easily be found, for this knowledge reveals its truth through itself when its revelations are not opposed by the human soul in the way indicated.[12]

In Egypt, quite a bit was written about these parts of us. The Egyptian version of the double was the *ka*. The ka was a part of the self that was spirit and immortal. It was said that when the physical body died, the ka separated and was sent on its mysterious journey of reincarnation. This immortal part of us lives within us our entire lives, residing in our flesh. The separation of the ka at death is explained in the *Egyptian Book of the Dead* and is related through the tale of Isis and Osiris when Osiris is murdered. Set, the satanic or luciferian double of Osiris, who some scholars believe is his brother, murders Osiris and rends him to pieces, whereupon his ka leaves him. Many feel that Set is the same thing as the ka, and that Set became destructive to force a rebirth. This destructive force of Set is called the Angra Mainyu in the Zoroastrian traditions. The familiar spirit of the adversary tears things down in order to be reconstructed. Osiris is torn to pieces, and then Isis goes on a journey to the underworld to put him back together again so that he can be reborn in a purer form. The double is very related to the death process and could explain why many Europeans saw the double before someone's death or as a kind of ghostly apparition of ourselves that we can't see until it is too late.

In his great work on the subject, *Witches, Werewolves, and Fairies*, Claude Lecouteux sheds a fair amount of light on the double.

So man possesses Doubles, most often two of them. One, material and physical, has the power either to take on animal appearances or keep its human form; the other, spiritual and psychic, is also capable of metamorphosis, but appears mostly in dreams. These Doubles have the ability to reach the other world—or any place whatsoever in this world—in one or another of their forms. . . . Death liberates Doubles; the physical alter ego yields a ghost, and the psychic alter ego is transformed into a phantom.[13]

The double familiar spirit is an aspect of ourselves of which we are mostly unaware. Only a deep internal reflection can pry it from the darkness and make it visible.

Who Are Your
Familiar Spirits?

"This is my advice. I would not have the shadow of a coolness between the two whose intimacy I have been observing with the greatest pleasure, and in whose characters, there is so much general resemblance in true generosity and natural delicacy as to make the few slight differences, resulting principally from situation, no reasonable hindrance to a perfect friendship. I would not have the shadow of a coolness arise," he repeated, his voice sinking a little, "between the two dearest objects."

JANE AUSTEN, *MANSFIELD PARK*

We are all nursing our familiar spirits, whether we realize it or not. We hold them close to our breast as an infant we refuse to release. The thoughts and feelings we go through unconsciously in our day-to-day lives all belong to the familiar spirits. They dwell deep within our grave mounds, and the fairy queen releases them when we look away. You can call them habits, or visitors, guests or kin, but they form our realities and shape our worlds. Think carefully upon the ways and habits of the familiar to you.

Are your familiar spirits your own, or are they in your environments, stored in the lands and animals around you? Human beings have a hard time remembering where they come from. This comes as a stark realization when one attempts to recall the names of their great-grandparents, who they were and what they did. Perhaps some who have made the effort can recount their lineages, but for most of the general populace, we have forgotten. This forgetting extends back much further in time through cultures, nations, and races. All humans have to try to put the story of origins back together again by looking at one another's broken pieces, deaths, and births. It does seem truly that some kind of tower of Babylon occurred that caused every single group of people to lose the answer of humanity's birth origins, of our family tree. Perhaps through examining the myriad mythological religious and cultural answers to our deepest roots, we can pick out some kind of discernible pattern through all the confusion and inconsistency. What we include as our family is much too small and limited for the information our physical forms contain. One thing that becomes undeniably certain when placing all the origin stories together is that there are commonalities among them. When the light is shown on all we hold in common, we discover that strange beings reside there: in indigenous stories of the forefathers, sooner or later in the saga a divine intervention between "human" and "beyond human" occurs. In trying to find out who the parents of humanity are, we discover that they aren't just severed from us by country, race, or even species but are intergalactically or interdimensionally separate from us. That is a big chasm to cross. Think about how far you extend your family circle and if it is a stretch to consider the beasts as part of your heritage; imagine how much difficulty you will have merging in holy matrimony with the stars and celestial bodies of our vast and beautiful universe.

Notes

Chapter 1. The Witch's Familiar

1. Coleridge, *Letters, Conversations, and Recollections,* 89.
2. Cox, *Naming Day in the Garden of Eden.*
3. Griffith, *Hieratic Papyri from Kahun and Gurob,* 13ff.
4. Ayto, *Dictionary of Word Origins,* 180.
5. Grillot de Givry, *Witchcraft, Magic & Alchemy,* 97.
6. Eliade, *Shamanism,* 88.
7. Flotte and Bell, "Role of Skin Lesions."
8. Goodcole, *The Wonderful Discovery of Elizabeth Sawyer,* 387.

Chapter 2. Shamanic Totems, the Nagual, and the Black Cat

1. Castaneda, *Teachings of Don Juan,* 35.
2. Castaneda, *Tales of Power,* 140, 194.
3. Middleton, *Magic, Witchcraft, and Curing,* 71.
4. Cornelison, *Weyekin Stories.*
5. Aftandilian, *What Are the Animals to Us?,* 12.
6. Tomorad, "The End of Ancient Egyptian Religion."

Chapter 3. The Fetch, the Libido, the Celibate, and the Familiar

1. Freud, *General Introduction to Psychoanalysis,* 312.
2. Ayto, *Dictionary of Word Origins,* 221.
3. Couliano, *Eros and Magic in the Renaissance,* 97.
4. Ingham, *Psychological Anthropology Reconsidered,* 168.
5. Beattie, "Divination in Bunyoro Uganda."
6. Hughes, *Revival.*
7. Blundell, *Women in Ancient Greece.*

Chapter 4. Greek Belly-Talkers, Witches, Sibyls, and Priestesses

1. Kadari, "Necromancer of Endor," *Jewish Women's Archive* online Encyclopedia.
2. Du Bartas, *Divine Weeks of Josuah Sylvester.*
3. *Shorter Oxford English Dictionary.*
4. Greer and Mitchell, *The "Belly-Myther" of Endor,* xiv.
5. MaatRaAh, "Pagan Goddess of the Sibyl and Cybele Oracle."
6. Pearlman, *Tibetan Sacred Dance,* 94.

Chapter 5. Familiar Spirits in Judeo-Christianity

1. Seux, "Pope Says 'True Christians Must Reject Horoscopes, Occult.'"
2. Merriam-Webster, "Origin of 'Inaugurate.'"
3. Gatto, "Why the Pope Wears Red Shoes."
4. Dennis, *Encyclopedia of Jewish Myth, Magic and Mysticism.*
5. Matt, *Zohar,* 254n.

Chapter 6. Isis, Pandora, and the Angels of the East

1. Meagher, *Helen: Myth, Legend, and the Culture of Misogyny,* chapter 3.
2. Kirk, "Hesiod's Pandora, a Demoted Earth Goddess?," 118.
3. Wikman, *Pregnant Darkness: Alchemy and the Rebirth of Consciousness,* chapter 3.
4. Aristophanes, *Facsimile of the Codex.*

Chapter 7. The Witch Watchers

1. Osburn, *Better Living Through Alchemy.*
2. Buttenweiser, "Apocalyptic Literature, Neo-Hebraic."
3. Malachi, *Irin & Kaddishin.*
4. Swart, *Book of Immediate Magic,* 132.
5. Strong, *Strong's Greek and Hebrew Dictionary of the Bible,* H5892.
6. Hancock and Bauval, *Message of the Sphinx,* 5.
7. Halperin, *Faces of the Chariot,* 41.
8. Hawass, *Treasures of the Pyramids.*

Chapter 8. The Holy Spirit versus Succubi and Incubi

1. Philo, "Allegorical Laws, 3:219," *The Works of Philo.*
2. Eisenstein, "The Alphabet of Ben Sira," *Ozar Midrashim,* 35–49.

Chapter 9. Fairy Familiars

1. Gaffin, *Running with Fairies,* 4.
2. Walker, *Woman's Encyclopedia of Myths and Secrets,* 299.

3. Walker, *Woman's Encyclopedia of Myths and Secrets,* 298.

4. Harper, *Online Etymology Dictionary.*

5. Moore, *Folk-Lore of the Isle of Man,* 45.

6. Lytton, *The Poetical and Dramatic Works of Sir Edward Bulwer Lytton,* 275.

7. Beyer, *Singing to the Plants,* 131.

8. Beyer, *Singing to the Plants,* 130.

9. Eliade, *Shamanism,* 74–75.

10. Orekhie, *Biblical Dream Interpretations with Warfare Prayers.*

Chapter 10. Queen Mothers
and Dragon Kings in Chinese Legends

1. Cooper, *Chinese Alchemy,* 21.

2. Nevius, *China and the Chinese,* 166–67.

3. Kang, *Cult of the Fox,* 17.

4. Ji Yun, *Notebook from the Thatched Cottage of Close Scrutiny.*

5. Kang, *Cult of the Fox,* 20.

6. Wei-tsu, "On the Cult of the Four Sacred Animals," 1.

7. Ranjan and Chang, "Chinese Dragon Concept as a Spiritual Force," 66.

Chapter 11. The Rishi Families
and Guiding Guardians of India

1. Chisholm, "Asceticism," *Encyclopedia Britannica,* 718.

2. Blavatsky, *Secret Doctrine,* 605n.

3. Oman, *Mystics, Ascetics, and Saints of India,* 63–64.

4. Altman, *Deva Handbook,* 3.

Chapter 12. The Voices in Our Heads:
The Daimon, the Genius, and the Double

1. Platt, *Facing the Gods,* 236.

2. Harper, *Online Etymology Dictionary.*

3. Crowley, *Magick without Tears,* chapter 83.

4. Harper, *Online Etymology Dictionary.*

5. Fradenburgh, *Departed Gods,* 128.

6. Waite, *Hermetic Museum,* 12.

7. Orr, "Turned On."

8. Kingsford, *Clothed with the Sun,* 39.

9. Kingsford, *Clothed with the Sun,* 36.

10. Polyphilus, "Moon under Her Feet."

11. Couliano, *Eros and Magic in the Renaissance,* 31.

12. Steiner, "Luciferic and Ahrimanic in Relation to Man."

13. Lecouteux, *Witches, Werewolves, and Fairies,* 147.

Bibliography

Altman, Nathaniel. *The Deva Handbook: How to Work with Nature's Subtle Energies.* Rochester, Vt.: Destiny Books, 1995.

Aftandilian, Dave, ed. *What Are the Animals to Us? Approaches from Science, Religion, Folklore, Literature, and Art.* Knoxville: University of Tennessee Press, 2007.

Aristophanes. *Facsimile of the Codex Vanetus Marcianus 474.* Boston: Archaelogical Institute of America, 1902.

Austen, Jane. *Mansfield Park.* Reprint. London: Wordsworth Editions, 1998. First published 1814 by Thomas Egerton.

Ayto, John. *Dictionary of Word Origins: Histories of More Than 8,000 English-Language Words.* New York: Arcade Publishing, 1990.

Beattie, John. "Divination in Bunyoro Uganda." *Sociologus* 14, no. 1 (1964): 44–62.

Beyer, Stephan V. *Singing to the Plants: A Guide to Mesitzo Shamanism in the Upper Amazon.* Albuquerque: University of New Mexico Press, 2009.

Blake, William. *The Marriage of Heaven and Hell.* Boston: John W. Luce, 1925.

Blavatsky, H. P. *The Secret Doctrine: The Synthesis of Science, Religion, and Philosophy.* 2nd ed. London: Theosophical Company, 1888.

Blundell, Sue. *Women in Ancient Greece.* London: British Museum Press, 1995.

Bockris, Victor. *With William Burroughs: A Report from the Bunker.* Revised ed. New York: St. Martin's Griffin, 1996.

Burton, Robert. *The Anatomy of Melancholy.* New York: New York Review Books, 2001.

Buttenwieser, Moses. "Apocalyptic Literature, Neo-Hebraic." In *Jewish Encyclopedia.* 12 vols. Managing editor: Isidore Singer. New York: Funk and Wagnalls, 1901–1906. JewishEncyclopedia.com.

Castaneda, Carlos. *Tales of Power.* Reissue ed. New York: Washington Square Press, 1985.

————. *The Teachings of Don Juan: A Yaqui Way of Knowledge.* Reissue ed. New York: Washington Square Press, 1985.

Chisholm, Hugh, ed. "Asceticism." *The Encyclopedia Britannica: A Dictionary of Arts, Sciences, Literature and General Information.* Vol. 1. 11th ed. New York: Encyclopedia Britannica Co., 1910.

Coleridge, S. T. *Letters, Conversations, and Recollections of S. T. Coleridge.* London: Edward Moxon, 1836.

Connor, Steven. *Dumbstruck: A Cultural History of Ventriloquism.* 1st ed. Oxford, UK: Oxford University Press, 2001.

Cooper, Jean. *Chinese Alchemy: Taoism, the Power of Gold, and the Quest for Immortality.* Newburyport, Mass.: Weiser Books, 2016.

Cornelison, J. M. *Weyekin Stories: Titwatit Weyekishnim.* San Francisco: E. L. Mackey & Co., 1911.

Couliano, Ioan P. *Eros and Magic in the Renaissance.* Chicago: University of Chicago Press, 1980.

Cox, Edward Godfrey. *Naming Day in the Garden of Eden.* Seattle: University of Washington Chapbooks, 1930.

Critchley, Simon. *The Book of Dead Philosophers.* New York: Vintage, 2009.

Crowley, Aleister. *Magick without Tears.* 8th ed. Phoenix, Ariz.: New Falcon, 1991.

de Montfaucon, Bernard. *Antiquity Explained, and Represented in Sculptures.* Translated by David Humphreys. London: J. Tonson and J. Watts, 1721.

Dennis, Geoffrey. *The Encyclopedia of Jewish Myth, Magic and Mysticism.* Woodbury, Minn.: Llewellyn, 2007.

Dillmann, August. *Book of Enoch.* London: Forgotten Books, 2016.

Donne, John. "Song: Go and catch a falling star." Poetry Foundation website, accessed January 28, 2019.

Du Bartas, Guillaume de Saluste. *The Divine Weeks of Josuah Sylvester: Mainly Translated from the French of William de Saluste, Lord of the Bartas.* Waukesha, Wisc.: H. M. Youmans, 1908. First published 1608.

Eisenstein, J. D., ed. *Ozar Midrashim: A Library of Two Hundred Minor Midrashim.* Vol. 1. Reznick, Menschel and Co., 1928. First published 1915 by J. D. Eisenstein, New York.

Eliade, Mircea. *Shamanism: Archaic Techniques of Ecstasy.* Princeton, N.J.: Princeton University Press, 1974.

Essbaum, Jill Alexander. *Hausfrau.* Reprint. New York: Random House, 2015.

Evans-Wentz, W. Y. *The Fairy-Faith in Celtic Countries.* London and New York: H. Froude, 1911.

Ferlinghetti, Lawrence. "To the Oracle at Delphi." Spoken to the Oracle by the author at UNESCO's World Poetry Day, March 21, 2001.

Flotte T. J., and D. A. Bell. "Role of Skin Lesions in the Salem Witchcraft Trials." *American Journal of Dermatopathology* 11, no. 6 (Dec. 1989): 582–87.

Fradenburgh, Rev. J. N. *Departed Gods: The Gods of Our Fathers.* Cincinnati and New York: Cranston & Stowe and Hunt & Eaton, 1891.

Freud, Sigmund. *A General Introduction to Psychoanalysis.* Translated by G. Stanley Hall. New York: Boni and Liveright, 1920.

Gaffin, Dennis. *Running with the Fairies: Towards a Transpersonal Anthropology of Religion.* Newcastle upon Tyne, UK: Cambridge Scholars, 2013.

Gatto, Massimo. "Why the Pope Wears Red Shoes." *The New York Review of Books,* NYR Daily, March 12, 2013.

Goodcole, Henry. *The Wonderful Discovery of Elizabeth Sawyer, a Witch.* Reprint. New York: Garland, 1980. First published 1621.

Greer, Rowan A., and Margaret M. Mitchell. *The "Belly-Myther" of Endor: Interpretations of 1 Kingdoms 28 in the Early Church.* Vol. 16 of *Society of Biblical Literature Writings from the Greco-Roman World.* Atlanta, Ga.: Society of Biblical Literature, 2007.

Grey, Piers. *T.S. Eliot.* Upper Saddle River, N.J.: Prentice Hall/Harvester Wheatsheaf, 1981.

Griffith, F.Ll., ed. *Hieratic Papyri from Kahun and Gurob.* London: Bernard Quaritch, 1898.

Grillot de Givry, Emile. *Witchcraft, Magic & Alchemy.* Translated by J. Courtenay Locke. New York: Dover, 2009.

Hall, Manly P. *The Secret Teachings of All Ages.* Limited ed. Los Angeles: Philosophical Research Society, 1975.

Halperin, David. *The Faces of the Chariot: Early Jewish Responses to Ezekiel's Vision.* Tübingen, Germany: J. C. B. Mohr, 1988.

Hancock, Graham, and Robert Bauval. *The Message of the Sphinx: A Quest for the Hidden Legacy of Mankind.* New York: Three Rivers Press, 1996.

Harper, Douglas. *Online Etymology Dictionary.* Etymonline.com, 2000.

Hawass, Zahi. *The Treasures of the Pyramids.* Novara, Italy: White Star, 2003.

Heraclitus. *Fragments.* Translated by John Burnet, Arthur Fairbanks, and Kathleen Freeman. Epub, 2012.

Hughes, Thomas Hywel. *Revival: The New Psychology and Religious Experience.* Abingdon, UK: Routledge, 2017. First published 1933.

Ingham, John. *Psychological Anthropology Reconsidered.* Cambridge: Cambridge University Press, 1996

Jung, Carl. *Part 1: Archetypes and the Collective Unconscious.* Vol. 9 of *The Collected Works of C. G. Jung.* Translated by R. F. C. Hull. 2nd ed. New York: Princeton University Press, 1968.

Kadari, Tamar. "Necromancer of Endor: Midrash and Aggadah." In *Jewish Women: A Comprehensive Historical Encyclopedia*. Edited by Paula E. Hyman and Dalia Ofer. Jewish Women's Archive and Shalvi Publishing, 2009. Available on Jewish Women's Archive website.

Kang, Xiaofei. *The Cult of the Fox: Power, Gender, and Popular Religion in Late Imperial and Modern China*. New York: Columbia University Press, 2006.

Kingsford, Anna. *Clothed with the Sun*. London: John M. Watkins, 1889.

Kircher, Athanasius. *Oedipus Egytpicus*. Rome: V. Mascardi, 1652.

Kirk, Stan. "Hesiod's Pandora: A Demoted Earth Goddess? An Overview of the Scholarship." *Journal of the Institute for Language and Culture* 17 (2013): 111–24.

Knight, Richard Payne. *Sexual Symbolism: A History of Phallic Worship*. New York: Dover, 2006.

Krishnananda. *Master-Pupil Talks*. Bangalore Urban, Karnataka (India): Manasa Light Age Foundation, 2012.

Lecouteux, Claude. *Witches, Werewolves, and Fairies*. Rochester, Vt.: Inner Traditions, 2003.

Lumpkin, Joseph B. *The Gnostic Gospels of Philip, Mary Magdalene, and Thomas*. Blountsville, Ala.: Fifth Estate, 2006.

Lytton, Bulwer. *The Poetical and Dramatic Works of Sir Edward Bulwer Lytton*. Vol. 1. London: Chapman and Hall, 1852.

MaatRaAh. "Pagan Goddess of the Sibyl and Cybele Oracle." Sabrina Aset, Goddess.org, 2015.

Maier, Michael. *Atalanta Fugiens*. Oppenheim, Germany: Johann Theodor de Bry, 1618.

Malachi, Tau. "Irin & Kaddishin: Great Angels of Supernal Judgment." The Fellowship: Ecclesia Pistis Sophia, Sophian.org, 2013.

Matt, Daniel C. *The Zohar*. 1st ed. Bloomington: Stanford University Press, 2003.

McBeath, Alastair, and Andrei Dorian Gheorghe. "Meteor Beliefs Project: Meteorite Worship in the Ancient Greek and Roman Worlds." *WGN: The Journal of the International Meteor Organization* 33, no. 5 (2005): 135–44.

Meagher, Robert Emmet. *Helen: Myth, Legend, and the Culture of Misogyny*. New York: Continuum, 1995.

Merriam-Webster. "The Origin of 'Inaugurate': What Does 'Inaugurate' Have to Do with Interpreting Omens?" accessed February 1, 2019, Merriam-Webster website.

Middleton, John, ed. *Magic, Witchcraft, and Curing*. Austin: University of Texas Press, 1967.

Molitor, Ulrich. *De Laniis et Phitonicis Mulierbus*. Cologne, Germany: Johann Otmar, 1489.

Moore, A. W. *The Folk-Lore of the Isle of Man*. Facsimile ed. Somerset, UK: Llanerch Press, 1994. First published 1891.

Müller, F. Max, ed. *The Sacred Books of China: The Texts of Tâoism.* Translated by James Legge. Oxford, UK: Clarendon Press, 1891.

Münster, Sebastian. *Cosmographia Universalis.* Basel, Germany: Heinrich Petri, 1598. First published 1544.

Nevius, John Livingston. *China and the Chinese: A General Description of the Country* [. . .]. Philadelphia: Presbyterian Board of Publication, 1882.

Oman, John Campbell. *The Mystics, Ascetics, and Saints of India: A Study of Sadhuism, with an Account of the Yogis, Sanyasis, Bairagis, and Other Strange Hindu Sectarians.* London: T. Fisher Unwin, 1905.

Orekhie, Joshua. *Biblical Dream Interpretations with Warfare Prayers.* Self-published, Amazon Digital Services, 2018.

Orr, Allen H. "Turned On: A Revolution in the Field of Evolution?" *New Yorker Magazine,* October 24, 2005.

Osburn, Lynn. *Better Living Through Alchemy.* Self-published, Amazon Digital Services, 2011.

Paxson, Diana L. *The Essential Guide to Possession, Depossession & Divine Relationships.* San Francisco: Weiser Books, 2015.

Pearlman, Ellen. *Tibetan Sacred Dance: A Journey into the Religious and Folk Traditions.* Rochester, Vt.: Inner Traditions, 2002.

Philo. *The Works of Philo: Complete and Unabridged.* Translated by C. D. Yonge. Peabody, Mass.: Hendrickson, 1993.

Piggott, Stuart. *The Druids.* New York: Praeger, 1968.

Platt, Verity. *Facing the Gods: Epiphany and Representation in Graeco-Roman Art, Literature and Religion.* New York: Cambridge University Press, 2011.

Poe, Edgar Allan. *The Complete Works of Edgar Allan Poe.* Akron, Ohio: Werner, 1908.

Pollard, Edward Bagby. "Familiars." In *International Standard Bible Encyclopedia,* edited by James Orr. Grand Rapids, Mich.: Wm. B. Eerdmans, 1939.

Polyphilus, T. *The Moon under Her Feet: Being an Acclamation of Madam Dr. Anna Mary Bonus Kingsford.* Hermetic Library website, 2016.

Ranjan, DharmaKeerthi Sri, and Zhou Chang. "The Chinese Dragon Concept as a Spiritual Force of the Masses." *Sabaragamuwa University Journal* 9, no. 1 (Dec. 2010): 65–80.

Raziel. *Sefer Raziel HaMalakh (Book of Raziel the Angel).* Amsterdam: Chabad-Lubavitch Library, 1701.

Seux, Leo. "Pope Says 'True Christians Must Reject Horoscopes, Occult.'" *The Italian Insider.* 27 June 2017.

Shakespeare, William. *Hamlet.* New York: Simon & Schuster, 2004.

———. *Love's Labour's Lost.* Oxford, UK: Oxford University Press, 2002.

Shorter Oxford English Dictionary. 6th ed. New York: Oxford University Press, 2007.

Steiner, Rudolph. "The Luciferic and Ahrimanic in Relation to Man." *Journal, Das Reich* 3, no. 3 (1904).

Strong, James. *Strong's Greek and Hebrew Dictionary of the Bible*. Nashville, Tenn.: Nelson Reference & Electronic Pub., 1996.

Swart, Jacobus G. *The Book of Immediate Magic: Part 1*. Johannesburg, South Africa: Sangreal Sodality Press, 2015.

Tomorad, M. "The End of Ancient Egyptian Religion: The Prohibition of Paganism in Egypt from the Middle of the 4th to the Middle of the 6th century A.D." *The Journal of Egyptological Studies* IV (2015): 147–64.

Trungpa, Chögyam. *Cutting Through Spiritual Materialism*. Boston: Shambhala, 1973.

Tyson, Donald. *Sexual Alchemy: Magical Intercourse with Spirits*. St. Paul, Minn.: Llewellyn, 2000.

Valmiki. *The Yoga-Vasishtha Maharamayana of Valmiki*. Translated by Vihari-Lala Mitra. Calcutta, India: Kahinoor Press, 1891.

von Stolcenberg, Daniel Stolcius. *Viridarium Chymicum*. Frankfurt, Germany, 1624.

Waite, Arthur Edward. *The Hermetic Museum*. New York: Weiser Books, 1999.

Walker, Barbara G. *The Woman's Encyclopedia of Myths and Secrets*. New York: HarperOne, 1983.

Wei-tsu, Li. "On the Cult of the Four Sacred Animals." *Folklore Studies* 7 (1948): 1–94.

White, David Gordon. *Sinister Yogis*. 1st ed. Chicago: University of Chicago Press, 2010.

Wikman, Monika. *Pregnant Darkness: Alchemy and the Rebirth of Consciousness*. Newburyport, Mass.: Nicolas-Hays, 2005.

Worsfold, T. Cato. *The History of the Vestal Virgins of Rome*. Reprint. Whitefish, Mont.: Kessinger, 1942. First published 1934 by Rider & Co., London.

Yun, Ji. *Notebook from the Thatched Cottage of Close Scrutiny (Yuewei caotang biji)*. 1789.

Index